ISBN 978-0-266-26281-7
PIBN 10926236

# CONSTITUTION

OF THE

# Commonwealth of Massachusetts.

PUBLISHED IN CONFORMITY TO A RESOLVE OF THE LEGISLATURE
OF APRIL 26, 1853.

BY THE SECRETARY OF THE COMMONWEALTH.

BOSTON:
WHITE AND POTTER, PRINTERS TO THE STATE,
4 SPRING LANE.
1853.

*Resolve to provide for distributing Copies of the present Constitution throughout the Commonwealth.*

*Resolved,* That the secretary of the commonwealth be authorized and directed, as soon as practicable, to cause to be printed an edition of the constitution of the commonwealth of Massachusetts, in cheap pamphlet form, of the same number as that published annually of the laws and resolves passed at each session of the legislature, and to be apportioned and sent, in the same proportion and the same manner as the laws and resolves, to the several city and town clerks; with such instructions for the distribution of the same in the respective cities and towns throughout the commonwealth, as he may find to be expedient in order to secure prompt delivery thereof.

Approved, April 26, 1853.

# CONSTITUTION

OR

# FORM OF GOVERNMENT

FOR THE

# Commonwealth of Massachusetts.

---

### PREAMBLE.

**Objects** of Government. — Body politic, how formed. — Its nature.

---

## PART THE FIRST.

**Art. 1.** Equality and natural rights of all men.

**2.** Right and duty of public religious worship. — Protection therein.

**3.** Legislature empowered to compel provision for public worship; and to enjoin attendance thereon. — Exclusive right of electing religious teachers secured. — Option, as to whom parochial taxes may be paid, unless, &c. — All denominations equally protected. — Subordination of one sect to another prohibited.

**4.** Right of self-government secured.

**5.** Accountability of all officers, &c.

**6.** Services rendered to the public being the only title to peculiar privileges, hereditary offices are absurd and unnatural.

**7.** Objects of government; right of people to institute and change it.

**8.** Right of people to secure rotation in office.

**9.** All, having the qualifications prescribed, equally eligible to office.

Art. 10. Right of protection and duty of contribution correlative. — Taxation founded on consent. — Private property not to be taken for public uses without, &c.

11. Remedies, by recourse to the law, to be free, complete, and prompt.

12. Prosecutions regulated. — Right to trial by jury in criminal cases, except, &c.

13. Crimes to be proved in the vicinity.

14. Right of search and seizure regulated.

15. Right to trial by jury sacred, except, &c.

16. Liberty of the press.

17. Right to keep and bear arms. — Standing armies dangerous. — Military power subordinate to civil.

18. Moral qualifications for office. — Moral obligations of lawgivers and magistrates.

19. Right of people to instruct representatives and petition legislature.

20. Power to suspend the laws, or their execution. — When and by whom exercised.

21. Freedom of debate, &c., and reason thereof.

22. Frequent sessions, and objects thereof.

23. Taxation founded on consent.

24. Ex post facto laws prohibited.

25. Legislature not to convict of treason, &c.

26. Excessive bail or fines, and cruel punishments, prohibited.

ART. 27. No soldier to be quartered in any house, unless, &c.
28. Citizens exempt from law martial, unless, &c.
29. Judges of Supreme Judicial Court. — Tenure of their office. — Salaries.
30. Separation of executive, judicial, and legislative departments.

## PART THE SECOND.

### CHAPTER I.

#### SECTION 1.

ART. 1. Legislative department.
2. Governor's veto. — Bill may be passed by two thirds of each house, notwithstanding.
3. General Court may constitute judicatories, courts of record, &c. — Courts, &c., may administer oaths.
4. General Court may enact laws, &c., not repugnant to the constitution; may provide for the election or appointment of officers; prescribe their duties; impose taxes; duties and excises, to be disposed of for defence, protection, &c. — Valuation of estates, once in ten years, at least, while, &c.

#### SECTION 2.

ART. 1. Senate, number of, and by whom elected. — Counties to be districts until, &c.
2. Manner and time of choosing senators and counsellors. — Word "inhabitant," defined. — Selectmen to preside at town meetings. — Return of votes. — Inhabitants of unincorporated plantations, who pay state taxes, may vote. — Plantation meetings. — Assessors to notify, &c.
3. Governor and council to examine and count votes and issue summonses.
4. Senate to be final judges of elections, &c., of its own members. — Vacancies, how filled.
5. Qualifications of a senator.
6. Senate not to adjourn more than two days.
7. Shall choose its officers and establish its rules.
8. Shall try all impeachments. — Oaths. — Limitation of sentence
9. Quorum.

#### SECTION 3.

ART. 1. Representation of the people.
2. Representatives, by whom chosen.— Proviso as to towns having less than one hundred and fifty ratable polls. — Towns liable to fine, in case, &c. — Expense of travelling to and from the General Court, how paid.
3. Qualifications of a representative.
4. Qualifications of a voter.
5. Representatives, when chosen.
6. House alone can impeach.
7. House to originate all money bills.
8. Not to adjourn more than two days.
9. Quorum.
10. House to judge of returns, &c., of its own members; to choose its officers and establish its rules, &c. — May punish for certian offences. — Privileges of members.
11. Governor and Council may punish. — General limitations. — Trial may be by committee, or otherwise.

### CHAPTER II.

#### SECTION 1.

ART. 1. Governor. — His title.
2. To be chosen annually. — Qualifications.
3. To be chosen by the people, by a major vote. — How chosen, when no person has a majority.
4. Power of governor, and of governor and Council.
5. Same subject.
6. Governor and Council may adjourn General Court, in cases, &c., but not exceeding ninety days.
7. Governor to be commander-in-chief. — Limitation.
8. Governor and Council may pardon offences, except, &c. — But not before conviction.
9. All judicial officers, &c., how nominated and appointed.
10. Militia officers, how elected. — How commissioned. — Major generals, how appointed and commissioned. — Vacancies, how filled, in case, &c. — Officers, duly commissioned, how removed. — Adjutants, &c., how appointed. — Organization of militia.
11. Money, how drawn from the treasury, except, &c.
12. All public boards, &c., to make quarterly returns.

ART. 13. Salary of governor. — Salaries of justices of Supreme Judicial Court. — Salaries to be enlarged, if insufficient.

SECTION 2.

ART. 1. Lieutenant governor, his title and qualifications. — How chosen.
2. President of Council.— Lieutenant governor a member of, except, &c.
3. Lieutenant governor to be acting governor, in case, &c.

SECTION 3.

ART. 1. Council.
2. Number; from whom and how chosen. — If senators become counsellors, their seats to be vacated.
3. Rank of counsellors.
4. No district to have more than two.
5. Register of Council.
6. Council to exercise the power of governor, in case, &c.
7. Elections may be adjourned, until, &c. — Order thereof.

SECTION 4.

ART. 1. Secretary, &c., by whom and how chosen. — Treasurer, ineligible for more than five successive years.
2. Secretary to keep records, to attend the governor and Council, &c.

CHAPTER III.

ART. 1. Tenure of all commissioned officers to be expressed. — Judicial officers to hold office during good behavior, except, &c. — But may be removed on address.
2. Justices of Supreme Judicial Court to give opinions, when required.
3. Justices of the peace; tenure of their office.
4. Provisions for holding probate courts.
5. Provisions for determining causes of marriage, divorce, &c.

CHAPTER IV.

Delegates to Congress.

CHAPTER V.

SECTION 1.

ART. 1. Harvard College. — Powers, privileges, &c., of the president and fellows, confirmed.
2. All gifts, grants, &c., confirmed.
3. Who shall be overseers. — Power of alteration reserved to the legislature.

SECTION 2.

Duty of legislators and magistrates in all future periods.

CHAPTER VI.

ART. 1. Oaths, &c.
2. Plurality of offices prohibited to governor, &c., except, &c. — Incompatible offices. — Bribery, &c., operate disqualifications.
3. Value of money ascertained. — Property qualifications may be increased.
4. Provisions respecting commissions.
5. Provisions respecting writs.
6. Continuation of former laws, except, &c.
7. Benefit of habeas corpus secured, except, &c.
8. The enacting style.
9. Officers of former government continued until, &c.
10. Provision for revising constitution.
11. Provision for preserving and publishing this constitution.

AMENDMENTS.

ART. 1. Bill, &c., not approved within five days, not to become a law, if legislature adjourn in the mean time.
2. General Court empowered to charter cities. — Proviso.
3. Qualifications of voters for governor, lieutenant governor, senators, and representatives.
4. Notaries public, how appointed and removed. — Vacancies in the office of secretary and treasurer, how filled, in case, &c. — Commissary general may be appointed, in case, &c. — Militia officers, how removed.
5. Who may vote for captains and subalterns.
6. Oath to be taken by all officers; or affirmation, in case, &c.
7. Tests abolished.
8. Incompatibility of offices.
9. Amendments to constitution, how made.
10. Commencement of political year, and termination. — Meetings for choice of governor, lieutenant governor, &c., when to be held. — May be adjourned. — Article, when to go into operation. — Inconsistent provisions annulled.
11. Religious freedom established.

# CONSTITUTION.

## PREAMBLE.

Objects of government.

The end of the institution, maintenance, and administration of government is to secure the existence of the body politic; to protect it; and to furnish the individuals who compose it with the power of enjoying, in safety and tranquillity, their natural rights and the blessings of life: and whenever these great objects are not obtained, the people have a right to alter the government, and to take measures necessary for their safety, prosperity, and happiness.

Body politic, how formed.

Its nature.

The body politic is formed by a voluntary association of individuals; it is a social compact, by which the whole people covenants with each citizen, and each citizen with the whole people, that all shall be governed by certain laws for the common good. It is the duty of the people, therefore, in framing a constitution of government, to provide for an equitable mode of making laws, as well as for an impartial interpretation and a faithful execution of them; that every man may, at all times, find his security in them.

We, therefore, the people of Massachusetts, acknowledging, with grateful hearts, the goodness of the great Legislator of the universe in affording us, in the course of his providence, an opportunity, deliberately and peaceably, without fraud, violence, or surprise, of entering into an original, explicit, and solemn compact with each other; and of forming a new constitution of civil government for ourselves and posterity; and devoutly imploring his direction in so interesting a design, do agree upon, ordain, and establish the following *Declaration of Rights, and Frame of Government*, as the CONSTITUTION of the COMMONWEALTH of MASSACHUSETTS.

# PART THE FIRST.

## *A Declaration of the Rights of the Inhabitants of the Commonwealth of Massachusetts.*

**Equality and natural rights of all men.**

ART. I. ALL men are born free and equal, and have certain natural, essential, and unalienable rights; among which may be reckoned the right of enjoying and defending their lives and liberties; that of acquiring, possessing, and protecting property; in fine, that of seeking and obtaining their safety and happiness.

**Right and duty of public religious worship. Protection therein.**

II. IT is the right as well as the duty of all men in society, publicly, and at stated seasons, to worship the SUPREME BEING, the great Creator and Preserver of the universe. And no subject shall be hurt, molested, or restrained, in his person, liberty, or estate, for worshipping GOD in the manner and season most agreeable to the dictates of his own conscience; or for his religious profession or sentiments; provided he doth not disturb the public peace, or obstruct others in their religious worship.

**See amendments, Art. XI.**

III. As the happiness of a people, and the good order and preservation of civil government, essentially depend upon piety, religion, and morality; and as these cannot be generally diffused through a community but by the institution of the public worship of GOD, and of public instructions in piety, religion, and morality: Therefore, to promote their happiness, and to secure the good order and preservation of their government, the people of this commonwealth have a right to invest their legislature with power to authorize and require, and the legislature shall, from time to time, authorize and require, the several towns, parishes, precincts, and other bodies politic, or religious societies, to make suitable provision, at their own expense, for the institution of the public worship of GOD, and for the support and maintenance of public Protestant teachers of piety, religion, and morality, in all cases where such provision shall not be made voluntarily.

**Legislature empowered to compel provision for public worship;**

**and to enjoin attendance thereon. See amendments, Art. XI.**

AND the people of this commonwealth have also a right to, and do, invest their legislature with authority to enjoin upon all the subjects an attendance upon the instructions of the public teachers aforesaid, at stated times and seasons, if there be any on whose instructions they can conscientiously and conveniently attend.

Exclusive right of electing religious teachers secured.

PROVIDED notwithstanding, that the several towns, parishes, precincts, and other bodies politic, or religious societies, shall, at all times, have the exclusive right of electing their public teachers, and of contracting with them for their support and maintenance.

Option as to whom parochial taxes may be paid, unless, &c.

AND all moneys, paid by the subject to the support of public worship, and of the public teachers aforesaid, shall, if he require it, be uniformly applied to the support of the public teacher or teachers of his own religious sect or denomination, provided there be any on whose instructions he attends: otherwise it may be paid towards the support of the teacher or teachers of the parish or precinct in which the said moneys are raised.

See amendments, Art. XI.

All denominations equally protected.

Subordination of one sect to another prohibited.

AND every denomination of Christians, demeaning themselves peaceably, and as good subjects of the commonwealth, shall be equally under the protection of the law; and no subordination of any one sect or denominaiton to another shall ever be established by law.

Right of self-government secured.

IV. THE people of this commonwealth have the sole and exclusive right of governing themselves, as a free, sovereign, and independent state; and do, and forever hereafter shall, exercise and enjoy every power, jurisdiction, and right, which is not, or may not hereafter, be by them expressly delegated to the United States of America, in Congress assembled.

Accountability of all officers, &c.

V. ALL power residing originally in the people, and being derived from them, the several magistrates and officers of government, vested with authority, whether legislative, executive, or judicial, are their substitutes and agents, and are at all times accountable to them.

Services rendered to the public being the only title to peculiar privileges, hereditary offices are absurd and unnatural.

VI. No man, nor corporation, or association of men, have any other title to obtain advantages, or particular and exclusive privileges, distinct from those of the community, than what arises from the consideration of services rendered to the public; and this title being in nature neither hereditary, nor transmissible to children, or descendants, or relations by blood, the idea of a man being born a magistrate, lawgiver, or judge, is absurd and unnatural.

Objects of government; right of people to institute and change it.

VII. GOVERNMENT is instituted for the common good; for the protection, safety, prosperity, and happiness of the people; and not for the profit, honor, or private interest of any one man, family, or class of men: Therefore the people alone have an incontestible, unalienable, and indefeasible right to institute government; and to reform, alter, or totally change the same, when their protection, safety, prosperity, and happiness require it.

Right of people to secure rotation in office.

VIII. IN order to prevent those who are vested with authority from becoming oppressors, the people have a right, at such periods and in such manner as they shall establish by their frame of government, to cause their public officers to return to private life; and to fill up vacant places by certain and regular elections and appointments.

All, having the qualifications prescribed, equally eligible to office.

IX. ALL elections ought to be free; and all the inhabitants of this commonwealth, having such qualifications as they shall establish by their frame of government, have an equal right to elect officers, and to be elected, for public employments.

Right of protection and duty of contribution correlative.

X. EACH individual of the society has a right to be protected by it in the enjoyment of his life, liberty, and property, according to standing laws. He is obliged, consequently, to contribute his share to the expense of this protection; to give his personal service, or an equivalent, when necessary: but no part of the property of any individual can, with justice, be taken from him or applied to public uses without his own consent, or that of the representative body of the people. In fine, the people of this commonwealth are not controlable by any other laws than those to which their constitutional representative body have given their consent. And whenever the public exigencies require that the property of any individual should be appropriated to public uses, he shall receive a reasonable compensation therefor.

Taxation founded on consent.

Private property not to be taken for public uses without, &c.

Remedies, by recourse to the law, to be free, complete, and prompt.

XI. EVERY subject of the commonwealth ought to find a certain remedy, by having recourse to the laws, for all injuries or wrongs which he may receive in his person, property, or character. He ought to obtain right and justice freely, and without being obliged to purchase it; completely, and without any denial; promptly, and without delay; conformably to the laws.

Prosecutions regulated.

XII. No subject shall be held to answer for any crimes or offence until the same is fully and plainly, substantially and formally, described to him; or be compelled to accuse or furnish evidence against himself; and every subject shall have a right to produce all proofs that may be favorable to him; to meet the witnesses against him face to face, and to be fully heard in his defence by himself, or his counsel, at his election: and no subject shall be arrested, imprisoned, despoiled, or deprived of his property, immunities, or privileges, put out of the protection of the law, exiled, or deprived of his life, liberty, or estate, but by the judgment of his peers, or the law of the land.

Right to trial by jury, in criminal cases, except, &c.

AND the legislature shall not make any law that shall subject any person to a capital or infamous punishment, excepting for the government of the army and navy, without trial by jury.

Crimes to be proved in the vicinity.

XIII. IN criminal prosecutions, the verification of facts, in the vicinity where they happen, is one of the greatest securities of the life, liberty, and property of the citizen.

Right of search and seizure regulated.

XIV. EVERY subject has a right to be secure from all unreasonable searches and seizures of his person, his houses, his papers, and all his possessions. All warrants, therefore, are contrary to this right, if the cause or foundation of them be not previously supported by oath or affirmation, and if the order in the warrant to a civil officer, to make search in suspected places, or to arrest one or more suspected persons, or to seize their property, be not accompanied with a special designation of the persons or objects of search, arrest, or seizure; and no warrant ought to be issued but in cases, and with the formalities, prescribed by the laws.

Right to trial by jury sacred, except, &c.

XV. IN all controversies concerning property, and in all suits between two or more persons, except in cases in which it has heretofore been otherways used and practised, the parties have a right to a trial by jury; and this method of procedure shall be held sacred, unless, in causes arising on the high seas, and such as relate to mariners' wages, the legislature shall hereafter find it necessary to alter it.

Liberty of the press.

XVI. THE liberty of the press is essential to the security of freedom in a state: it ought not, therefore, to be restrained in this commonwealth.

XVII. THE people have a right to keep and to bear arms for the common defence; and, as in time of peace, armies are dangerous to liberty, they ought not to be maintained without the consent of the legislature; and the military power shall always be held in an exact subordination to the civil authority, and be governed by it.

Right to keep and bear arms. Standing armies dangerous. Military power subordinate to civil.

XVIII. A FREQUENT recurrence to the fundamental principles of the constitution, and a constant adherence to those of piety, justice, moderation, temperance, industry, and frugality, are absolutely necessary to preserve the advantages of liberty, and to maintain a free government. The people ought, consequently, to have a particular attention to all those principles, in the choice of their officers and representatives; and they have a right to require of their lawgivers and magistrates an exact and constant observance of them, in the formation and execution of the laws necessary for the good administration of the commonwealth.

Moral qualifications for office.

Moral obligations of lawgivers and magistrates.

XIX. THE people have a right, in an orderly and peaceable manner, to assemble to consult upon the common good, give instructions to their representatives, and to request of the legislative body, by the way of addresses, petitions, or remonstrances, redress of the wrongs done them, and of the grievances they suffer.

Right of people to instruct representatives and petition legislature.

XX. THE power of suspending the laws, or the execution of the laws, ought never to be exercised but by the legislature, or by authority derived from it, to be exercised in such particular cases only as the legislature shall expressly provide for.

Power to suspend the laws or their execution.

XXI. THE freedom of deliberation, speech, and debate, in either house of the legislature, is so essential to the rights of the people, that it cannot be the foundation of any accusation or prosecution, action or complaint, in any other court or place whatsoever.

Freedom of debate, &c., and reason thereof.

XXII. THE legislature ought frequently to assemble for the redress of grievances, for correcting, strengthening, and confirming the laws, and for making new laws, as the common good may require.

Frequent sessions, and objects thereof.

XXIII. No subsidy, charge, tax, impost, or duties ought to

Taxation founded on consent.

be established, fixed, laid, or levied, under any pretext whatsoever, without the consent of the people, or their representatives in the legislature.

Ex post facto laws prohibited.

XXIV. LAWS made to punish for actions done before the existence of such laws, and which have not been declared crimes by preceding laws, are unjust, oppressive, and inconsistent with the fundamental principles of a free government.

Legislature not to convict of treason, &c.

XXV. No subject ought, in any case, or in any time, to be declared guilty of treason or felony by the legislature.

Excessive bail or fines, and cruel punishments, prohibited.

XXVI. No magistrate or court of law shall demand excessive bail or sureties, impose excessive fines, or inflict cruel or unusual punishments.

No soldier to be quartered in any house, unless, &c.

XXVII. IN time of peace, no soldier ought to be quartered in any house without the consent of the owner; and in time of war, such quarters ought not to be made but by the civil magistrate, in a manner ordained by the legislature.

Citizens exempt from law-martial, unless, &c.

XXVIII. No person can in any case be subjected to law martial, or to any penalties or pains, by virtue of that law, except those employed in the army or navy, and except the militia in actual service, but by authority of the legislature.

Judges of Supreme Judicial Court.

XXIX. IT is essential to the preservation of the rights of every individual, his life, liberty, property, and character, that there be an impartial interpretation of the laws, and administration of justice. It is the right of every citizen to be tried by judges as free, impartial, and independent as the lot of humanity will admit. It is, therefore, not only the best policy,

Tenure of their office.

but for the security of the rights of the people, and of every citizen, that the judges of the Supreme Judicial Court should hold their offices as long as they behave themselves well, and that they should have honorable salaries ascertained and estab-

Salaries.

lished by standing laws.

Separation of executive, judicial, and legislative departments.

XXX. IN the government of this commonwealth, the legislative department shall never exercise the executive and judicial powers, or either of them: the executive shall never exercise the legislative and judicial powers, or either of them: the judicial shall never exercise the legislative and executive powers, or either of them; to the end it may be a government of laws, and not of men.

---

# PART THE SECOND.

*The Frame of Government.*

THE people, inhabiting the territory formerly called the Province of Massachusetts Bay, do hereby solemnly and mutually agree with each other, to form themselves into a free, sovereign, and independent body politic or state, by the name of THE COMMONWEALTH OF MASSACHUSETTS.

## CHAPTER I.

### THE LEGISLATIVE POWER.

#### SECTION I.

*The General Court.*

ART. I. THE department of legislation shall be formed by two branches, a Senate and House of Representatives; each of which shall have a negative on the other. Legislative department.

THE legislative body shall assemble every year, on the last Wednesday in May, and at such other times as they shall judge necessary; and shall dissolve and be dissolved on the day next preceding the said last Wednesday in May; and shall be styled THE GENERAL COURT OF MASSACHUSETTS. See amendments, Art. X.

II. No bill or resolve of the Senate or House of Representatives shall become a law, and have force as such, until it shall have been laid before the governor for his revisal; and if he, upon such revision, approve thereof, he shall signify his approbation by signing the same. But if he have any objection to the passing of such bill or resolve, he shall return the same, together with his objections thereto, in writing, to the Senate or House of Representatives, in whichsoever the same shall Governor's veto.

have originated, who shall enter the objections sent down by the governor, at large, on their records, and proceed to reconsider the said bill or resolve: but if, after such reconsideration, two thirds of the said Senate or House of Representatives shall, notwithstanding the said objections, agree to pass the same, it shall, together with the objections, be sent to the other branch of the legislature, where it shall also be reconsidered, and if approved by two thirds of the members present, shall have the force of a law: but in all such cases, the votes of both houses shall be determined by yeas and nays; and the names of the persons voting for, or against, the said bill or resolve, shall be entered upon the public records of the commonwealth.

Bill may be passed by two thirds of each house, notwithstanding.

AND, in order to prevent unnecessary delays, if any bill or resolve shall not be returned by the governor within five days after it shall have been presented, the same shall have the force of a law.

See amendments, Art. I.

III. THE General Court shall forever have full power and authority to erect and constitute judicatories and courts of record, or other courts, to be held in the name of the commonwealth, for the hearing, trying, and determining of all manner of crimes, offences, pleas, processes, plaints, actions, matters, causes, and things, whatsoever, arising or happening within the commonwealth, or between or concerning persons inhabiting, or residing, or brought within the same; whether the same be criminal or civil, or whether the said crimes be capital or not capital, and whether the said pleas be real, personal, or mixed; and for the awarding and making out of execution thereupon: to which courts and judicatories are hereby given and granted full power and authority, from time to time, to administer oaths or affirmations, for the better discovery of truth in any matter in controversy, or depending before them.

General Court may constitute judicatories, courts of record, &c.

Courts, &c., may administer oaths.

IV. AND further, full power and authority are hereby given and granted to the said General Court, from time to time, to make, ordain, and establish all manner of wholesome and reasonable orders, laws, statutes, and ordinances, directions, and instructions, either with penalties or without, so as the same be not repugnant or contrary to this constitution, as they shall judge to be for the good and welfare of this commonwealth, and for the government and ordering thereof, and of the sub-

General Court may enact laws, &c., not repugnant to the constitution;

jects of the same, and for the necessary support and defence of the government thereof; and to name and settle annually, or provide by fixed laws for the naming and settling, all civil officers within the said commonwealth, the election and constitution of whom are not hereafter in this form of government otherwise provided for; and to set forth the several duties, powers, and limits, of the several civil and military officers of this commonwealth, and the forms of such oaths or affirmations as shall be respectively administered unto them for the execution of their several offices and places, so as the same be not repugnant or contrary to this constitution; and to impose and levy proportional and reasonable assessments, rates, and taxes upon all the inhabitants of, and persons resident, and estates lying, within the said commonwealth; and also to impose and levy reasonable duties and excises upon any produce, goods, wares, merchandise, and commodities whatsoever, brought into, produced, manufactured, or being within the same; to be issued and disposed of by warrant, under the hand of the governor of this commonwealth for the time being, with the advice and consent of the Council, for the public service, in the necessary defence and support of the government of the said commonwealth, and the protection and preservation of the subjects thereof, according to such acts as are or shall be in force within the same.

may provide for the election or appointment of officers;

prescribe their duties;

impose taxes;

duties and excises;

to be disposed of for defence, protection, &c.

AND while the public charges of government, or any part thereof, shall be assessed on polls and estates, in the manner that has hitherto been practised, in order that such assessments may be made with equality, there shall be a valuation of estates within the commonwealth, taken anew once in every ten years at least, and as much oftener as the General Court shall order.

Valuation of estates once in ten years, at least, while, &c.

---

# CHAPTER I.

## SECTION II.

### *Senate.*

ART. I. THERE shall be annually elected, by the freeholders and other inhabitants of this commonwealth, qualified as in this constitution is provided, forty persons to be counsellors

Senate, number of, and by whom elected.

and senators, for the year ensuing their election; to be chosen by the inhabitants of the districts, into which the commonwealth may from time to time be divided by the General Court for that purpose: and the General Court, in assigning the numbers to be elected by the respective districts, shall govern themselves by the proportion of the public taxes paid by the said districts; and timely make known to the inhabitants of the commonwealth the limits of each district, and the number of counsellors and senators to be chosen therein; provided, that the number of such districts shall never be less than thirteen; and that no district be so large as to entitle the same to choose more than six senators.

Counties to be districts until, &c.

AND the several counties in this commonwealth shall, until the General Court shall determine it necessary to alter the said districts, be districts for the choice of counsellors and senators, (except that the counties of Dukes county and Nantucket shall form one district for that purpose,) and shall elect the following number for counsellors and senators, viz.: —

| | | | |
|---|---|---|---|
| Suffolk | six. | York | two. |
| Essex | six. | Dukes county and Nantucket | one. |
| Middlesex | five. | Worcester | five. |
| Hampshire | four. | Cumberland | one. |
| Plymouth | three. | Lincoln | one. |
| Barnstable | one. | Berkshire | two. |
| Bristol | three. | | |

Manner and time of choosing senators and counsellors.

See amendments, Art. II. and X.

II. THE Senate shall be the first branch of the legislature; and the senators shall be chosen in the following manner, viz.: there shall be a meeting on the first Monday in April annually, forever, of the inhabitants of each town in the several counties of this commonwealth, to be called by the selectmen, and warned in due course of law, at least seven days before the first Monday in April, for the purpose of electing persons to be senators and counsellors; and at such meetings every male inhabitant of twenty-one years of age and upwards, having a freehold estate, within the commonwealth, of the annual income of three pounds, or any estate of the value of sixty pounds, shall have a right to give in his vote for the senators for the district of which he is an inhabitant. And to remove all doubts concerning the meaning of the word "inhabitant," in this constitution, every person shall be considered as an inhabitant, for the purpose of electing and being elected into any office, or place within this state, in that town, district, or plantation, where he dwelleth, or hath his home.

See amendments, Art. III.

Word "inhabitant" defined.

THE selectmen of the several towns shall preside at such meetings impartially, and shall receive the votes of all the inhabitants of such towns present and qualified to vote for senators, and shall sort and count them in open town meeting, and in presence of the town clerk, who shall make a fair record, in presence of the selectmen, and in open town meeting, of the name of every person voted for, and of the number of votes against his name; and a fair copy of this record shall be attested by the selectmen and the town clerk, and shall be sealed up, directed to the secretary of the commonwealth for the time being, with a superscription expressing the purport of the contents thereof, and delivered by the town clerk of such towns to the sheriff of the county in which such town lies, thirty days at least before the last Wednesday in May annually; or it shall be delivered into the secretary's office seventeen days at least before the said last Wednesday in May; and the sheriff of each county shall deliver all such certificates, by him received, into the secretary's office, seventeen days before the said last Wednesday in May.

Selectmen to preside at town meetings.

Return of votes.

See amendments, Art. II and X.

AND the inhabitants of plantations unincorporated, qualified as this constitution provides, who are or shall be empowered and required to assess taxes upon themselves toward the support of government, shall have the same privilege of voting for counsellors and senators, in the plantations where they reside, as town inhabitants have in their respective towns; and the plantation meetings for that purpose shall be held annually on the same first Monday in April, at such place in the plantations respectively as the assessors thereof shall direct; which assessors shall have like authority for notifying the electors, collecting and returning the votes, as the selectmen and town clerks have in their several towns, by this constitution. And all other persons living in places unincorporated, (qualified as aforesaid,) who shall be assessed to the support of government, by the assessors of an adjacent town, shall have the privilege of giving in their votes for counsellors and senators, in the town where they shall be assessed, and be notified of the place of meeting by the selectmen of the town where they shall be assessed, for that purpose, accordingly.

Inhabitants of unincorporated plantations, who pay state taxes, may vote.

Plantation meetings.

See amendments, Art. X.

Assessors to notify, &c.

III. AND that there may be a due convention of senators on the last Wednesday in May annually, the governor, with five of the Council, for the time being, shall, as soon as may be, examine the returned copies of such records; and fourteen

Governor and Council to examine and count votes, and issue summonses.

See amendments, Art. X.

days before the said day, he shall issue his summons to such persons as shall appear to be chosen by a majority of voters, to attend on that day, and take their seats accordingly: provided, nevertheless, that for the first year, the said returned copies shall be examined by the president and five of the Council of the former constitution of government; and the said president shall, in like manner, issue his summons to the persons so elected, that they may take their seats as aforesaid.

Senate to be final judge of elections, &c., of their own members.

See amendments, Art. X.

IV. THE Senate shall be the final judge of the elections, returns, and qualifications of their own members, as pointed out in the constitution; and shall, on the said last Wednesday in May annually, determine and declare who are elected by each district to be senators, by a majority of votes: and in case there shall not appear to be the full number of senators returned, elected by a majority of votes for any district, the deficiency shall be supplied in the following manner, viz.: The members of the House of Representatives, and such senators as shall be declared elected, shall take the names of such persons as shall be found to have the highest number of votes in such district, and not elected, amounting to twice the number of senators wanting, if there be so many voted for; and, out of these, shall elect by ballot a number of senators sufficient to fill up the vacancies in such district; and in this manner all such vacancies shall be filled up in every district of the commonwealth; and in like manner all vacancies in the Senate, arising by death, removal out of the state, or otherwise, shall be supplied as soon as may be after such vacancies shall happen.

Vacancies, how filled.

Qualifications of a senator.

V. PROVIDED, nevertheless, that no person shall be capable of being elected as a senator, who is not seized in his own right of a freehold, within this commonwealth, of the value of three hundred pounds at least, or possessed of personal estate to the value of six hundred pounds at least, or of both to the amount of the same sum, and who has not been an inhabitant of this commonwealth for the space of five years immediately preceding his election, and, at the time of his election, he shall be an inhabitant in the district for which he shall be chosen.

Senate not to adjourn more than two days.

VI. THE Senate shall have power to adjourn themselves, provided such adjournments do not exceed two days at a time.

VII. The Senate shall choose its own president, appoint its own officers, and determine its own rules of proceeding. Shall choose its officers, and establish its rules.

VIII. The Senate shall be a court, with full authority, to hear and determine all impeachments made by the House of Representatives, against any officer or officers of the commonwealth, for misconduct and mal-administration in their offices: but, previous to the trial of every impeachment, the members of the Senate shall respectively be sworn, truly and impartially to try and determine the charge in question, according to evidence. Their judgment, however, shall not extend further than to removal from office, and disqualification to hold or enjoy any place of honor, trust, or profit, under this commonwealth: but the party so convicted shall be, nevertheless, liable to indictment, trial, judgment, and punishment, according to the laws of the land. Shall try all impeachments. Oath. Limitation of sentence.

IX. Not less than sixteen members of the Senate shall constitute a quorum for doing business. Quorum.

---

## CHAPTER I.

### SECTION III.

*House of Representatives.*

Art. I. There shall be, in the legislature of this commonwealth, a representation of the people, annually elected, and founded upon the principle of equality. Representation of the people.

II. And in order to provide for a representation of the citizens of this commonwealth, founded upon the principle of equality, every corporate town, containing one hundred and fifty ratable polls, may elect one representative; every corporate town, containing three hundred and seventy-five ratable polls, may elect two representatives; every corporate town, containing six hundred ratable polls, may elect three representatives; and proceeding in that manner, making two hundred and twenty-five ratable polls the mean increasing number for every additional representative. Representatives, by whom chosen

Proviso as to towns having less than 150 ratable polls.

PROVIDED, nevertheless, that each town now incorporated, not having one hundred and fifty ratable polls, may elect one representative; but no place shall hereafter be incorporated with the privilege of electing a representative, unless there are within the same one hundred and fifty ratable polls.

Towns liable to fine in case, &c.

AND the House of Representatives shall have power, from time to time, to impose fines upon such towns as shall neglect to choose and return members to the same, agreeably to this constitution.

Expense of travelling to and from the General Court, how paid.

THE expenses of travelling to the general assembly, and returning home, once in every session, and no more, shall be paid by the government, out of the public treasury, to every member who shall attend as seasonably as he can in the judgment of the house, and does not depart without leave.

Qualifications of a representative.

III. EVERY member of the House of Representatives shall be chosen by written votes; and, for one year at least next preceding his election, shall have been an inhabitant of, and have been seized in his own right of, a freehold of the value of one hundred pounds, within the town he shall be chosen to represent, or any ratable estate to the value of two hundred pounds; and he shall cease to represent the said town, immediately on his ceasing to be qualified as aforesaid.

Qualifications of a voter.

See amendments, Art. III.

IV. EVERY male person, being twenty-one years of age, and resident in any particular town in this commonwealth for the space of one year next preceding, having a freehold estate, within the same town, of the annual income of three pounds, or any estate of the value of sixty pounds, shall have a right to vote in the choice of a representative or representatives for the said town.

Representatives, when chosen. See amendment, Art. X.

V. THE members of the House of Representatives shall be chosen annually in the month of May, ten days at least before the last Wednesday of that month.

House alone can impeach.

VI. THE House of Representatives shall be the grand inquest of this commonwealth; and all impeachments made by them shall be heard and tried by the Senate.

House to originate all money bills.

VII. ALL money bills shall originate in the House of Representatives; but the Senate may propose or concur with amendments, as on other bills.

VIII. The House of Representatives shall have power to adjourn themselves, provided such adjournment shall not exceed two days at a time.

Not to adjourn more than two days.

IX. Not less than sixty members of the House of Representatives shall constitute a quorum for doing business.

Quorum.

X. The House of Representatives shall be judge of the returns, elections, and qualifications of its own members, as pointed out in the constitution; shall choose their own speaker, appoint their own officers, and settle the rules and orders of proceeding in their own house. They shall have authority to punish by imprisonment every person, not a member, who shall be guilty of disrespect to the house, by any disorderly or contemptuous behavio in its presence; or who, in the town where the General Court is sitting, and during the time of its sitting, shall threaten harm to the body or estate of any of its members, for any thing said or done in the House; or who shall assault any of them therefor; or who shall assault, or arrest, any witness, or other person ordered to attend the House, in his way in going or returning; or who shall rescue any person arrested by the order of the house.

House to judge of returns, &c. of its own members, To choose its officers and establish its rules, &c. May punish for certain offences.

And no member of the House of Representatives shall be arrested, or held to bail on mean process, during his going unto, returning from, or his attending, the general assembly.

Privileges of members.

XI. The Senate shall have the same powers in the like cases; and the governor and Council shall have the same authority to punish in like cases: provided, that no imprisonment, on the warrant or order of the governor, Council, Senate, or House of Representatives, for either of the above described offences, be for a term exceeding thirty days.

Governor and council may punish

General limitation.

And the Senate and House of Representatives may try, and determine, all cases where their rights and privileges are concerned, and which, by the constitution, they have authority to try and determine, by committees of their own members, or in such other way as they may respectively think best.

Trial may be by committee, or otherwise.

## CHAPTER II.

### EXECUTIVE POWER.

### SECTION I.

*Governor.*

Governor

His title.

ART. I. THERE shall be a supreme executive magistrate, who shall be styled — THE GOVERNOR OF THE COMMONWEALTH OF MASSACHUSETTS; and whose title shall be — HIS EXCELLENCY.

To be chosen annually.
Qualifications.

II. THE governor shall be chosen annually; and no person shall be eligible to this office, unless, at the time of his election, he shall have been an inhabitant of this commonwealth for seven years next preceding; and unless he shall, at the same time, be seized, in his own right, of a freehold, within the commonwealth, of the value of one thousand pounds; and unless he shall declare himself to be of the Christian religion.

See amendments, Art. VII.

By whom chosen, if he have a majority of votes.

See amendments, Art. II. and X.

III. THOSE persons who shall be qualified to vote for senators and representatives, within the several towns of this commonwealth, shall, at a meeting to be called for that purpose, on the first Monday of April annually, give in their votes for a governor, to the selectmen, who shall preside at such meetings; and the town clerk, in the presence and with the assistance of the selectmen, shall, in open town meeting, sort and count the votes, and form a list of the persons voted for, with the number of votes for each person against his name; and shall make a fair record of the same in the town books, and a public declaration thereof in the said meeting; and shall, in the presence of the inhabitants, seal up copies of the said list, attested by him and the selectmen, and transmit the same to the sheriff of the county, thirty days at least before the last Wednesday in May; and the sheriff shall transmit the same to the secretary's office seventeen days at least before the said last Wednesday in May; or the selectmen may cause returns of the same to be made to the office of the secretary of the commonwealth seventeen days at least before the said day · and the secretary shall lay the same before the Senate and the House of Representatives, on the last Wednesday in May, to be by them examined; and in case of an election by a majority of all the votes returned, the choice shall be by them declared and published; but if no person shall have a majority of votes, the House of Representatives shall, by ballot, elect two out of four persons, who had the highest number of votes, if so many shall have been voted for; but, if otherwise, out of the number voted for; and make return to the Senate of the two persons so elected; on which the Senate shall proceed, by ballot, to elect one, who shall be declared governor.

How chosen, when no person has a majority.

IV. THE governor shall have authority, from time to time, at his discretion, to assemble and call together the counsellors of this commonwealth for the time being; and the governor, with the said counsellors, or five of them at least, shall, and may, from time to time, hold and keep a Council, for the ordering and directing the affairs of the commonwealth, agreeably to the constitution and the laws of the land..

Power of governor, and of governor and Council.

V. THE governor, with advice of Council, shall have full power and authority, during the session of the General Court, to adjourn or prorogue the same to any time the two houses shall desire; and to dissolve the same on the day next preceding the last Wednesday in May; and, in the recess of the said court, to prorogue the same from time to time, not exceeding ninety days in any one recess; and to call it together sooner than the time to which it may be adjourned or prorogued, if the welfare of the commonwealth shall require the same; and in case of any infectious distemper prevailing in the place where the said court is next at any time to convene, or any other cause happening, whereby danger may arise to the health or lives of the members from their attendance, he may direct the session to be held at some other the most convenient place within the state.

Same subject.

See amendments, Art. X.

AND the governor shall dissolve the said General Court on the day next preceding the last Wednesday in May.

See amendments, Art. X.

VI. IN cases of disagreement between the two houses, with regard to the necessity, expediency, or time of adjournment, or prorogation, the governor, with advice of the Council, shall have a right to adjourn or prorogue the General Court, not exceeding ninety days, as he shall determine the public good shall require.

Governor and Council may adjourn General Court in cases, &c., but not exceeding 90 days

VII. THE governor of this commonwealth, for the time

Governor to be commander-in chief.

being, shall be the commander-in-chief of the army and navy, and of all the military forces of the state, by sea and land; and shall have full power, by himself, or by any commander, or other officer or officers, from time to time, to train, instruct, exercise, and govern the militia and navy; and, for the special defence and safety of the commonwealth, to assemble in martial array, and put in warlike posture, the inhabitants thereof, and to lead and conduct them, and with them to encounter, repel, resist, expel, and pursue, by force of arms, as well by sea as by land, within or without the limits of this commonwealth, and also to kill, slay, and destroy, if necessary, and conquer, by all fitting ways, enterprises, and means whatsoever, all and every such person and persons as shall, at any time hereafter, in a hostile manner, attempt or enterprise the destruction, invasion, detriment, or annoyance of this commonwealth; and to use and exercise, over the army and navy, and over the militia in actual service, the law martial, in time of war or invasion, and also in time of rebellion, declared by the legislature to exist, as occasion shall necessarily require; and to take and surprise, by all ways and means whatsoever, all and every such person or persons, with their ships, arms, ammunition, and other goods, as shall in a hostile manner invade, or attempt the invading, conquering, or annoying this commonwealth; and that the governor be intrusted with all these and other powers, incident to the offices of captain general and commander-in-chief, and admiral, to be exercised agreeably to the rules and regulations of the constitution, and the laws of the land, and not otherwise.

Limitation.

PROVIDED, that the said governor shall not, at any time hereafter, by virtue of any power by this constitution granted, or hereafter to be granted to him by the legislature, transport any of the inhabitants of this commonwealth, or oblige them to march out of the limits of the same, without their free and voluntary consent, or the consent of the General Court; except so far as may be necessary to march or transport them by land or water, for the defence of such part of the state to which they cannot otherwise conveniently have access.

Governor and Council may pardon offences, except, &c.

VIII. THE power of pardoning offences, except such as persons may be convicted of before the Senate, by an impeachment of the House, shall be in the governor, by and with the advice of Council; but no charter of pardon, granted by the governor, with advice of the Council, before conviction,

But not before conviction.

shall avail the party pleading the same, notwithstanding any general or particular expressions contained therein, descriptive of the offence or offences intended to be pardoned.

All judicial officers, &c., how nominated and appointed.

IX. ALL judicial officers, the attorney general, the solicitor general, all sheriffs, coroners, and registers of probate, shall be nominated and appointed by the governor, by and with the advice and consent of the Council; and every such nomination shall be made by the governor, and made at least seven days prior to such appointment.

Militia officers, how elected. See amendments, Art. V.

X. THE captains and subalterns of the militia shall be elected by the written votes of the train band and alarm list of their respective companies, of twenty-one years of age and upwards; the field officers of regiments shall be elected, by the written votes of the captains and subalterns of their respective regiments; the brigadiers shall be elected, in like manner, by the field officers of their respective brigades; and such officers, so elected, shall be commissioned by the governor, who shall determine their rank.

How commissioned.

THE legislature shall, by standing laws, direct the time and manner of convening the electors, and of collecting votes, and of certifying to the governor the officers elected.

Major generals, how appointed and commissioned.

THE major generals shall be appointed by the Senate and House of Representatives, each having a negative upon the other; and be commissioned by the governor.

Vacancies, how filled, in case &c.

AND if the electors of brigadiers, field officers, captains or subalterns, shall neglect or refuse to make such elections, after being duly notified, according to the laws for the time being, then the governor, with advice of Council, shall appoint suitable persons to fill such offices.

Officers, duly commissioned, how removed. See amendments, Art. IV.

AND no officer, duly commissioned to command in the militia, shall be removed from his office, but by the address of both houses to the governor, or by fair trial in court martial, pursuant to the laws of the commonwealth for the time being.

Adjutants, &c. how appointed.

THE commanding officers of regiments shall appoint their adjutants and quarter masters; the brigadiers their brigade majors; and the major generals their aids; and the governor shall appoint the adjutant general.

THE governor, with advice of Council, shall appoint all officers of the continental army, whom by the confederation of the United States it is provided that this commonwealth shall appoint, — as also all officers of forts and garrisons.

Organization of militia.

THE divisions of the militia into brigades, regiments, and companies, made in pursuance of the militia laws now in force, shall be considered as the proper divisions of the militia of this commonwealth, until the same shall be altered in pursuance of some future law.

Money, how drawn from the treasury, except, &c.

XI. No moneys shall be issued out of the treasury of this commonwealth and disposed of (except such sums as may be appropriated for the redemption of bills of credit or treasurer's notes, or for the payment of interest arising thereon) but by warrant under the hand of the governor for the time being, with the advice and consent of the Council, for the necessary defence and support of the commmonwealth, and for the protection and preservation of the inhabitants thereof, agreeably to the acts and resolves of the General Court.

All public boards, &c. to make quarterly returns.

XII. ALL public boards, the commissary general, all superintending officers of public magazines and stores, belonging to this commonwealth, and all commanding officers of forts and garrisons within the same, shall, once in every three months, officially and without requisition, and at other times, when required by the governor, deliver to him an account of all goods, stores, provisions, ammunition, cannon with their appendages, and small arms with their accoutrements, and of all other public property whatever under their care respectively; distinguishing the quantity, number, quality, and kind of each, as particularly as may be; together with the condition of such forts and garrisons; and the said commanding officer shall exhibit to the governor, when required by him, true and exact plans of such forts, and of the land and sea, or harbor or harbors adjacent.

AND the said boards, and all public officers, shall communicate to the governor, as soon as may be after receiving the same, all letters, despatches, and intelligences of a public nature, which shall be directed to them respectively.

Salary of governor.

XIII. As the public good requires that the governor should not be under the undue influence of any of the members of the General Court, by a dependence on them for his support — that he should, in all cases, act with freedom for the benefit of the public — that he should not have his attention necessarily diverted from that object to his private concerns — and that he should maintain the dignity of the commonwealth in the character of its chief magistrate — it is necessary that he should have an honorable stated salary, of a fixed and permanent value, amply sufficient for those purposes, and established by standing laws: and it shall be among the first acts of the General Court, after the commencement of this constitution, to establish such salary by law accordingly.

PERMANENT and honorable salaries shall also be established by law for the justices of the Supreme Judicial Court. Salaries of justices of Supreme Judicial Court.

AND if it shall be found, that any of the salaries aforesaid, so established, are insufficient, they shall, from time to time, be enlarged, as the General Court shall judge proper. Salaries to be enlarged, if insufficient.

---

## CHAPTER II.

### SECTION II.

*Lieutenant Governor.*

ART. I. THERE shall be annually elected a lieutenant governor of the commonwealth of Massachusetts, whose title shall be—HIS HONOR; and who shall be qualified, in point of religion, property, and residence in the commonwealth, in the same manner with the governor; and the day and manner of his election, and the qualifications of the electors, shall be the same as are required in the election of a governor. The return of the votes for this officer, and the declaration of his election, shall be in the same manner; and if no one person shall be found to have a majority of all the votes returned, the vacancy shall be filled by the Senate and House of Representatives, in the same manner as the governor is to be elected, in case no one person shall have a majority of the votes of the people to be governor. Lieutenant governor; his title and qualifications. See amendments, Art. III VI. and X. How chosen.

II. THE governor, and in his absence the lieutenant governor, shall be president of the Council, but shall have no vote in Council; and the lieutenant governor shall always be a member of the Council, except when the chair of the governor shall be vacant. President of Council. Lt. governor a member of, except, &c.

III. WHENEVER the chair of the governor shall be vacant, by reason of his death, or absence from the commonwealth, or otherwise, the lieutenant governor, for the time being, shall, Lieutenant governor to be acting governor, in case, &c.

during such vacancy, perform all the duties incumbent upon the governor, and shall have and exercise all the powers and authorities which, by this constitution, the governor is vested with, when personally present.

---

## CHAPTER II.

### SECTION III.

*Council, and the Manner of settling Elections by the Legislature.*

Council.

ART. I. THERE shall be a Council for advising the governor in the executive part of the government, to consist of nine persons besides the lieutenant governor, whom the governor, for the time being, shall have full power and authority, from time to time, at his discretion, to assemble and call together; and the governor, with the said counsellors, or five of them at least, shall and may, from time to time, hold and keep a Council, for the ordering and directing the affairs of the commonwealth, according to the laws of the land.

Number; from whom and how chosen.

See amendments, Art. X.

II. NINE counsellors shall be annually chosen from among the persons returned for counsellors and senators, on the last Wednesday in May, by the joint ballot of the senators and representatives assembled in one room; and in case there shall not be found, upon the first choice, the whole number of nine persons who will accept a seat in the Council, the deficiency shall be made up by the electors aforesaid from among the people at large; and the number of senators left, shall constitute the Senate for the year. The seats of the persons thus elected from the Senate, and accepting the trust, shall be vacated in the Senate.

If senators become counsellors their seats to be vacated.

Rank of counsellors.

III. THE counsellors, in the civil arrangements of the commonwealth, shall have rank next after the lieutenant governor.

No district to have more than two.

IV. NOT more than two counsellors shall be chosen out of any one district of this commonwealth.

Register of Council.

V. THE resolutions and advice of the Council shall be recorded in a register, and signed by the members present; and this record may be called for at any time by either house of the legislature; and any member of the Council may insert his opinion contrary to the resolution of the majority.

VI. WHENEVER the office of the governor and lieutenant governor shall be vacant, by reason of death, absence, or otherwise, then the Council, or the major part of them, shall, during such vacancy, have full power and authority to do, and execute, all and every such acts, matters, and things, as the governor or the lieutenant governor might or could, by virtue of this constitution, do or execute, if they, or either of them, were personally present.

Council to exercise the power of governor, in case, &c.

VII. AND whereas the elections appointed to be made by this constitution, on the last Wednesday in May annually, by the two houses of the legislature, may not be completed on that day, the said elections may be adjourned from day to day, until the same shall be completed. And the order of elections shall be as follows: the vacancies in the Senate, if any, shall first be filled up; the governor and lieutenant governor shall then be elected, provided there should be no choice of them by the people; and afterwards the two houses shall proceed to the election of the Council.

Elections may be adjourned, until, &c.

Order thereof.

---

## CHAPTER II.

### SECTION IV.

*Secretary, Treasurer, Commissary, &c.*

ART. I. THE secretary, treasurer and receiver general, and the commissary general, notaries public, and naval officers, shall be chosen annually by joint ballot of the senators and representatives in one room; and, that the citizens of this commonwealth may be assured, from time to time, that the moneys remaining in the public treasury, upon the settlement and liquidation of the public accounts, are their property, no man shall be eligible as treasurer and receiver general more than five years successively.

Secretary, &c.; by whom and how chosen.

See amendments, Art. IV.

Treasurer, ineligible for more than five successive years.

Secretary to keep records, to attend the governor and Council, &c.

II. THE records of the commonwealth shall be kept in the office of the secretary, who may appoint his deputies, for whose conduct he shall be accountable, and he shall attend the governor and Council, the Senate and House of Representatives, in person, or by his deputies, as they shall respectively require.

---

## CHAPTER III.

### JUDICIARY POWER.

Tenure of all commissioned officers to be expressed. Judicial officers to hold office during good behavior, except, &c. But may be removed on address.

ART. I. THE tenure, that all commission officers shall by law have in their offices, shall be expressed in their respective commissions. All judicial officers, duly appointed, commissioned, and sworn, shall hold their offices during good behavior, excepting such concerning whom there is different provision made in this constitution; provided, nevertheless, the governor, with consent of the Council, may remove them upon the address of both houses of the legislature.

Justices of Supreme Judicial Court to give opinions when required.

II. EACH branch of the legislature, as well as the governor and Council, shall have authority to require the opinions of the justices of the Supreme Judicial Court, upon important questions of law, and upon solemn occasions.

Justices of the peace; tenure of their office.

III. IN order that the people may not suffer from the long continuance in place of any justice of the peace, who shall fail of discharging the important duties of his office with ability or fidelity, all commissions of justices of the peace shall expire and become void in the term of seven years from their respective dates; and, upon the expiration of any commission, the same may, if necessary, be renewed, or another person appointed, as shall most conduce to the well being of the commonwealth.

Provisions for holding Probate Courts.

IV. THE judges of probate of wills, and for granting letters of administration, shall hold their courts at such place or places, on fixed days, as the convenience of the people shall require; and the legislature shall, from time to time hereafter, appoint such times and places; until which appointments, the said courts shall be holden at the times and places which the respective judges shall direct.

V. ALL causes of marriage, divorce, and alimony, and all appeals from the judges of probate, shall be heard and determined by the governor and Council, until the legislature shall, by law, make other provision. Provisions for determining causes of marriage, divorce, &c.

---

## CHAPTER IV.

### DELEGATES TO CONGRESS.

THE delegates of this commonwealth to the Congress of the United States shall, some time in the month of June, annually, be elected by the joint ballot of the Senate and House of Representatives, assembled together in one room; to serve in Congress for one year, to commence on the first Monday in November then next ensuing. They shall have commissions under the hand of the governor, and the great seal of the commonwealth, but may be recalled at any time within the year, and others chosen and commissioned, in the same manner, in their stead. Delegates to Congress.

---

## CHAPTER V.

### THE UNIVERSITY AT CAMBRIDGE, AND ENCOURAGEMENT OF LITERATURE, &C.

#### SECTION I.

*The University.*

ART. I. WHEREAS our wise and pious ancestors, so early as the year one thousand six hundred and thirty-six, laid the foundation of Harvard College, in which university many persons of great eminence have, by the blessing of GOD, been Harvard College.

initiated in those arts and sciences which qualified them for public employments, both in church and state; and whereas the encouragement of arts and sciences, and all good literature, tends to the honor of GOD, the advantage of the Christian religion, and the great benefit of this and the other United States of America, — it is declared, that the PRESIDENT AND FELLOWS OF HARVARD COLLEGE, in their corporate capacity, and their successors in that capacity, their officers and servants, shall have, hold, use, exercise, and enjoy, all the powers, authorities, rights, liberties, privileges, immunities, and franchises, which they now have, or are entitled to have, hold, use, exercise, and enjoy; and the same are hereby ratified and confirmed unto them, the said president and fellows of Harvard College, and to their successors, and to their officers and servants, respectively, forever.

Powers, privileges, &c., of the president and fellows confirmed.

II. AND whereas there have been, at sundry times, by divers persons, gifts, grants, devises of houses, lands, tenements, goods, chattels, legacies, and conveyances, heretofore made, either to Harvard College in Cambridge, in New England, or to the president and fellows of Harvard College, or to the said college by some other description, under several charters successively; it is declared, that all the said gifts, grants, devises, legacies, and conveyances, are hereby forever confirmed unto the president and fellows of Harvard College, and to their successors, in the capacity aforesaid, according to the true intent and meaning of the donor or donors, grantor or grantors, devisor or devisors.

All gifts, grants, &c., confirmed.

III. AND whereas by an act of the General Court of the colony of Massachusetts Bay, passed in the year one thousand six hundred and forty-two, the governor and deputy governor, for the time being, and all the magistrates of that jurisdiction, were, with the president, and a number of the clergy in the said act described, constituted the overseers of Harvard College; and it being necessary, in this new constitution of government, to ascertain who shall be deemed successors to the said governor, deputy governor, and magistrates; it is declared, that the governor, lieutenant governor, Council, and Senate of this commonwealth are, and shall be deemed, their successors; who, with the president of Harvard College, for the time being, together with the ministers of the congregational churches in the towns of Cambridge, Watertown,

Who shall be overseers.

Charlestown, Boston, Roxbury, and Dorchester, mentioned in the said act, shall be, and hereby are, vested with all the powers and authority belonging, or in any way appertaining, to the overseers of Harvard College; provided, that nothing herein shall be construed to prevent the legislature of this commonwealth from making such alterations in the government of the said university, as shall be conducive to its advantage, and the interest of the republic of letters, in as full a manner as might have been done by the legislature of the late province of the Massachusetts Bay.

Power of alteration reserved to the legislature.

---

## CHAPTER V.

### SECTION II.

*The Encouragement of Literature, &c.*

WISDOM and knowledge, as well as virtue, diffused generally among the body of the people, being necessary for the preservation of their rights and liberties, and as these depend on spreading the opportunities and advantages of education in the various parts of the country, and among the different orders of the people, it shall be the duty of legislatures and magistrates, in all future periods of this commonwealth, to cherish the interests of literature and the sciences, and all seminaries of them; especially the university at Cambridge, public schools, and grammar schools in the towns; to encourage private societies and public institutions, rewards and immunities, for the promotion of agriculture, arts, sciences, commerce, trades, manufactures, and a natural history of the country, to countenance and inculcate the principles of humanity and general benevolence, public and private charity, industry and frugality, honesty and punctuality in their dealings; sincerity, good humor, and all social affections, and generous sentiments among the people.

Duty of legislatures and magistrates in all future periods.

5

## CHAPTER VI.

OATHS AND SUBSCRIPTIONS; INCOMPATIBILITY OF AND EXCLUSION FROM OFFICES; PECUNIARY QUALIFICATIONS; COMMISSIONS; WRITS; CONFIRMATION OF LAWS; HABEAS CORPUS; THE ENACTING STYLE; CONTINUANCE OF OFFICERS; PROVISION FOR A FUTURE REVISAL OF THE CONSTITUTION, &c.

ART. I. ANY person chosen governor, lieutenant governor, counsellor, senator, or representative, and accepting the trust, shall, before he proceed to execute the duties of his place or office, make and subscribe the following declaration, viz.: —

See amendments, Art. VII.

"I, A. B., do declare, that I believe the Christian religion, and have a firm persuasion of its truth; and that I am seized and possessed, in my own right, of the property required by the constitution as one qualification for the office or place to which I am elected."

AND the governor, lieutenant governor, and counsellors, shall make and subscribe the said declaration, in the presence of the two houses of assembly; and the senators and representatives, first elected under this constitution, before the president and five of the Council of the former constitution, and forever afterwards, before the governor and Council for the time being.

AND every person, chosen to either of the places or offices aforesaid, as also any person appointed or commissioned to any judicial, executive, military, or other office under the government, shall, before he enters on the discharge of the business of his place or office, take and subscribe the following declaration, and oaths or affirmations, viz.: —

See amendment, Art. VI.

"I, A. B., do truly and sincerely acknowledge, profess, testify, and declare, that the commonwealth of Massachusetts is, and of right ought to be, a free, sovereign, and independent state; and I do swear, that I will bear true faith and allegiance to the said commonwealth, and that I will defend the same against traitorous conspiracies and all hostile attempts whatsoever; and that I do renounce and abjure all allegiance, subjection, and obedience to the king, queen, or government of Great Britain, (as the case may be,) and every other foreign power whatsoever; and that no foreign prince, person, prelate, state, or potentate hath, or ought to have, any jurisdiction, superiority, preëminence, authority, dispensing or other power, in any matter, civil, ecclesiastical or spiritual, within this commonwealth; except the authority and power which is or may be vested by their constituents in the Congress of the United States; and I do further testify and declare, that no man, or body of men, hath, or can have, any right to absolve or discharge me from the obligation of this oath, declaration, or affirmation; and that I do make this acknowledgment, profession, testimony, declaration, denial, renunciation, and abjuration, heartily and truly, according to the common meaning and acceptation of the foregoing words, without any equivocation, mental evasion, or secret reservation whatsoever. So help me GOD."

"I, A. B., do solemnly swear and affirm, that I will faithfully and impartially discharge and perform all the duties incumbent on me as , according to the best of my abilities and understanding, agreeably to the rules and regulations of the constitution, and the laws of the commonwealth. So help me GOD."

PROVIDED always, that when any person, chosen or appointed as aforesaid, shall be of the denomination of the people called Quakers, and shall decline taking the said oaths, he shall make his affirmation in the foregoing form, and subscribe the same, omitting the words "*I do swear,*" "*and abjure,*" "*oath or,*" "*and abjuration,*" in the first oath; and in the second oath, the words "*swear and,*" and in each of them the words "*So help me* GOD;" subjoining instead thereof, "*This I do under the pains and penalties of perjury.*"

AND the said oaths or affirmations shall be taken and subscribed by the governor, lieutenant governor, and counsellors, before the president of the Senate, in the presence of the two houses of assembly; and by the senators and representatives first elected under this constitution, before the president and five of the Council of the former constitution; and forever afterwards before the governor and Council for the time being; and by the residue of the officers aforesaid, before such persons, and in such manner, as from time to time shall be prescribed by the legislature.

Plurality of offices prohibited to governor, &c., except, &c.

II. No governor, lieutenant governor, or judge of the Supreme Judicial Court, shall hold any other office or place, under the authority of this commonwealth, except such as by this constitution they are admitted to hold, saving that the judges of the said court may hold the offices of justices of the peace through the state; nor shall they hold any other place or office, or receive any pension or salary from any other state, or government, or power whatever.

Same subject.

No person shall be capable of holding or exercising at the same time, within this state, more than one of the following offices, viz.: judge of probate — sheriff — register of probate — or register of deeds; and never more than any two offices, which are to be held by appointment of the governor, or the governor and Council, or the Senate, or the House of Representatives, or by the election of the people of the state at large, or of the people of any county, military offices, and the offices of justices of the peace excepted, shall be held by one person.

Incompatible offices.

See amendments, Art. VIII.

No person holding the office of judge of the Supreme Judicial Court — secretary — attorney general — solicitor general — treasurer or receiver general — judge of probate — commissary general — president, professor, or instructor of Harvard College — sheriff — clerk of the House of Representatives — register of probate — register of deeds — clerk of the Supreme Judicial Court — clerk of the inferior Court of Common Pleas — or officer of the customs, including in this description naval officers — shall at the same time have a seat in the Senate or House of Representatives; but their being chosen or appointed to and accepting the same shall operate as a resignation of their seat in the Senate or House of Representatives; and the place so vacated shall be filled up.

Same subject.

And the same rule shall take place in case any judge of the said Supreme Judicial Court, or judge of probate, shall accept a seat in Council; or any counsellor shall accept of either of those offices or places.

Bribery, &c., operates disqualification.

And no person shall ever be admitted to hold a seat in the legislature, or any office of trust or importance under the government of this commonwealth, who shall, in the due course of law, have been convicted of bribery or corruption in obtaining an election or appointment.

Value of money ascertained.

III. In all cases, where sums of money are mentioned in this constitution, the value thereof shall be computed in silver, at six shillings and eight pence per ounce; and it shall be in the power of the legislature, from time to time, to increase such qualifications, as to property, of the persons to be elected to offices, as the circumstances of the commonwealth shall require.

Property qualifications may be increased.

IV. All commissions shall be in the name of the commonwealth of Massachusetts, signed by the governor, and attested by the secretary or his deputy, and have the great seal of the commonwealth affixed thereto.

Provisions respecting commissions.

V. All writs, issuing out of the clerk's office in any of the courts of law, shall be in the name of the commonwealth of Massachusetts; they shall be under the seal of the court from whence they issue; they shall bear test of the first justice of the court to which they shall be returnable, who is not a party, and be signed by the clerk of such court.

Provisions respecting writs.

VI. All the laws, which have heretofore been adopted, used, and approved, in the province, colony, or state of Massachusetts Bay, and usually practised on in the courts of law, shall still remain and be in full force, until altered or repealed by the legislature; such parts only excepted as are repugnant to the rights and liberties contained in this constitution.

Continuation of former laws, except, &c.

VII. The privilege and benefit of the writ of *habeas corpus* shall be enjoyed in this commonwealth, in the most free, easy, cheap, expeditious, and ample manner; and shall not be suspended by the legislature, except upon the most urgent and pressing occasions, and for a limited time, not exceeding twelve months.

Benefit of habeas corpus secured, except, &c.

VIII. The enacting style, in making and passing all acts, statutes, and laws, shall be, "Be it enacted by the Senate and House of Representatives, in General Court assembled, and by the authority of the same."

The enacting style.

IX. To the end there may be no failure of justice, or danger, arise to the commonwealth, from a change of the form of government, all officers, civil and military, holding commissions under the government and people of Massachusetts Bay, in New England, and all other officers of the said government and people, at the time this constitution shall take effect, shall have, hold, use, exercise, and enjoy all the powers and authority to them granted or committed, until other persons shall be appointed in their stead; and all courts of law shall proceed in the execution of the business of their respective departments; and all the executive and legislative officers, bodies, and powers shall continue in full force, in the enjoyment and

Officers of former government continued until, &c.

exercise of all their trusts, employments, and authority, until the General Court, and the supreme and executive officers under this constitution, are designated, and invested with their respective trusts, powers, and authority.

Provision for revising constitution.

X. In order the more effectually to adhere to the principles of the constitution, and to correct those violations which by any means may be made therein, as well as to form such alterations as from experience shall be found necessary, the General Court, which shall be in the year of our Lord one thousand seven hundred and ninety-five, shall issue precepts to the selectmen of the several towns, and to the assessors of the unincorporated plantations, directing them to convene the qualified voters of their respective towns and plantations, for the purpose of collecting their sentiments on the necessity or expediency of revising the constitution, in order to amendments.

Same subject.

And if it shall appear, by the returns made, that two thirds of the qualified voters throughout the state, who shall assemble and vote in consequence of the said precepts, are in favor of such revision or amendment, the General Court shall issue precepts, or direct them to be issued from the secretary's office, to the several towns, to elect delegates to meet in convention, for the purpose aforesaid.

The said delegates to be chosen in the same manner and proportion as their representatives in the second branch of the legislature are by this constitution to be chosen.

Provision for preserving and publishing this constitution.

XI. This form of government shall be enrolled on parchment, and deposited in the secretary's office, and be a part of the laws of the land ; and printed copies thereof shall be prefixed to the book containing the laws of this commonwealth, in all future editions of the said laws.

---

## ARTICLES OF AMENDMENT.

Bill, &c., not approved within five days, not to become a law, if legislature adjourn in the mean time.

Art. 1. If any bill or resolve shall be objected to, and not approved by the governor, and if the General Court shall adjourn within five days after the same shall have been laid before the governor, for his approbation, and thereby prevent his returning it, with his objections, as provided by the constitution, such bill or resolve shall not become a law, nor have force as such.

ART. 2. THE General Court shall have full power and authority to erect and constitute municipal or city governments, in any corporate town or towns in this commonwealth, and to grant to the inhabitants thereof such powers, privileges, and immunities, not repugnant to the constitution, as the General Court shall deem necessary or expedient for the regulation and government thereof, and to prescribe the manner of calling and holding public meetings of the inhabitants in wards, or otherwise, for the election of officers under the constitution, and the manner of returning the votes given at such meetings: provided, that no such government shall be erected or constituted in any town not containing twelve thousand inhabitants, nor unless it be with the consent, and on the application, of a majority of the inhabitants of such town, present and voting thereon, pursuant to a vote at a meeting duly warned and holden for that purpose: and provided, also, that all by-laws, made by such municipal or city government, shall be subject, at all times, to be annulled by the General Court.

**General Court empowered to charter cities.**

**Proviso.**

ART. 3. EVERY male citizen of twenty-one years of age and upwards, (excepting paupers and persons under guardianship,) who shall have resided within the commonwealth one year, and within the town or district, in which he may claim a right to vote, six calendar months next preceding any election of governor, lieutenant governor, senators, or representatives, and who shall have paid, by himself or his parent, master, or guardian, any state or county tax, which shall, within two years next preceding such election, have been assessed upon him, in any town or district of this commonwealth; and also every citizen who shall be by law exempted from taxation, and who shall be in all other respects qualified as above mentioned, shall have a right to vote in such election of governor, lieutenant governor, senators, and representatives; and no other person shall be entitled to vote in such elections.

Qualifications of voters for governor, lieutenant governor, senators, and representatives. 11 Pick. 538.

ART. 4. NOTARIES public shall be appointed by the governor, in the same manner as judicial officers are appointed, and shall hold their offices during seven years, unless sooner

**Notaries public, how appointed and removed.**

removed by the governor, with the consent of the Council, upon the address of both houses of the legislature.

Vacancies in the office of secretary and treasurer, how filled, in case, &c.

In case the office of secretary or treasurer of the commonwealth shall become vacant from any cause, during the recess of the General Court, the governor, with the advice and consent of the Council, shall nominate and appoint, under such regulations as may be prescribed by law, a competent and suitable person to such vacant office, who shall hold the same until a successor shall be appointed by the General Court.

Commissary general may be appointed, in case, &c.

Whenever the exigencies of the commonwealth shall require the appointment of a commissary general, he shall be nominated, appointed, and commissioned, in such manner as the legislature may, by law, prescribe.

Militia officers, how removed.

All officers commissioned to command in the militia, may be removed from office in such manner as the legislature may, by law, prescribe.

Who may vote for captains and subalterns.

Art. 5. In the elections of captains and subalterns of the militia, all the members of their respective companies, as well those under, as those above the age of twenty-one years, shall have a right to vote.

Oath to be taken by all officers;

Art. 6. Instead of the oath of allegiance prescribed by the constitution, the following oath shall be taken and subscribed by every person chosen or appointed to any office, civil or military, under the government of this commonwealth, before he shall enter on the duties of his office, to wit: —

"I, A. B., do solemnly swear, that I will bear true faith and allegiance to the commonwealth of Massachusetts, and will support the constitution thereof. So help me God."

or affirmation in case, &c.

*Provided*, That when any person shall be of the denomination called Quakers, and shall decline taking said oath, he shall make his affirmation in the foregoing form, omitting the word "swear," and inserting, instead thereof, the word "affirm," and omitting the words "So help me God," and subjoining, instead thereof, the words "This I do under the pains and penalties of perjury."

Tests abolished.

Art. 7. No oath, declaration, or subscription, excepting the oath prescribed in the preceding article, and the oath of office, shall be required of the governor, lieutenant governor, counsellors, senators, or representatives, to qualify them to perform the duties of their respective offices.

Incompatibility of offices.

ART. 8. No judge of any court of this commonwealth, (except the Court of Sessions,) and no person holding any office under the authority of the United States, (postmasters excepted,) shall, at the same time, hold the office of governor, lieutenant governor, or counsellor, or have a seat in the Senate or House of Representatives of this commonwealth; and no judge of any court in this commonwealth, (except the Court of Sessions,) nor the attorney general, solicitor general, county attorney, clerk of any court, sheriff, treasurer and receiver general, register of probate, nor register of deeds, shall continue to hold his said office after being elected a member of the Congress of the United States, and accepting that trust; but the acceptance of such trust, by any of the officers aforesaid, shall be deemed and taken to be a resignation of his said office; and judges of the Courts of Common Pleas shall hold no other office under the government of this commonwealth, the office of justice of the peace and militia offices excepted.

Amendments to constitution, how made.

ART. 9. IF, at any time hereafter, any specific and particular amendment or amendments to the constitution be proposed in the General Court, and agreed to by a majority of the senators and two thirds of the members of the House of Representatives present and voting thereon, such proposed amendment or amendments shall be entered on the journals of the two houses, with the yeas and nays taken thereon, and referred to the General Court then next to be chosen, and shall be published; and if in the General Court next chosen, as aforesaid, such proposed amendment or amendments shall be agreed to by a majority of the senators and two thirds of the members of the House of Representatives present and voting thereon, then it shall be the duty of the General Court to submit such proposed amendment or amendments to the people; and if they shall be approved and ratified by a majority of the qualified voters, voting thereon, at meetings legally warned and holden for that purpose, they shall become part of the constitution of this commonwealth.

Commencement of political year

ART. 10. THE political year shall begin on the first Wednesday of January, instead of the last Wednesday of May, and the General Court shall assemble every year on the said first Wednesday of January, and shall proceed, at that session, to make all the elections, and do all the other acts, which are by the constitution required to be made and done at the session which has heretofore commenced on the last Wednesday of May And the General Court shall be dissolved on the day next preceding the first Wednesday of January, without any proclamation or other act of the governor. But nothing herein contained shall prevent the General Court from assembling at such other times as they shall judge necessary, or when called together by the governor. The governor, lieutenant governor, and counsellors shall also hold their respective offices for one year next following the first Wednesday of January, and until others are chosen and qualified in their stead.

and termination.

Meetings for choice of governor, lieutenant governor, &c., when to be held.

THE meeting for the choice of governor, lieutenant governor, senators, and representatives shall be held on the second Monday of November in every year; but meetings may be adjourned, if necessary, for the choice of representatives, to the next day, and again to the next succeeding day, but no further. But in case a second meeting shall be necessary for the choice of representatives, such meetings shall be held on the fourth Monday of the same month of November.

May be adjourned.

ALL the other provisions of the constitution, respecting the elections and proceedings of the members of the General Court, or of any other officers or persons whatever, that have reference to the last Wednesday of May as the commencement of the political year, shall be so far altered as to have like reference to the first Wednesday of January.

Article, when to go into operation.

THIS article shall go into operation on the first day of October, next following the day when the same shall be duly ratified and adopted as an amendment of the constitution; and the governor, lieutenant governor, counsellors, senators, representatives, and all other state officers, who are annually chosen, and who shall be chosen for the current year, when the same shall go into operation, shall hold their respective offices until the first Wednesday of January then next following, and until others are chosen and qualified in their stead, and no longer; and the first election of the governor, lieutenant governor, senators, and representatives, to be had in virtue of this article, shall be had conformably thereunto, in the month of November following the day on which the same shall be in force and go into operation, pursuant to the foregoing provision.

Inconsistent provisions annulled.

ALL the provisions of the existing constitution, inconsistent with the provisions herein contained, are hereby wholly annulled.

ART. 11. Instead of the third article of the bill of rights, the following modification and amendment thereof is substituted : —

Religious freedom established.

As the public worship of God, and instructions in piety, religion, and morality, promote the happiness and prosperity of a people, and the security of a republican government, therefore the several religious societies of this commonwealth, whether corporate or unincorporate, at any meeting legally warned and holden for that purpose, shall ever have the right to elect their pastors or religious teachers, to contract with them for their support, to raise money for erecting and repairing houses for public worship, for the maintenance of religious instruction, and for the payment of necessary expenses: And all persons belonging to any religious society shall be taken and held to be members, until they shall file with the clerk of such society a written notice declaring the dissolution of their membership, and thenceforth shall not be liable for any grant or contract which may be thereafter made or entered into by such society: And all religious sects and denominations, demeaning themselves peaceably, and as good citizens of the commonwealth, shall be equally under the protection of the law; and no subordination of any one sect or denomination to another shall ever be established by law.

ART. 12. In order to provide for a representation of the citizens of this commonwealth, founded upon the principles of equality, a census of the ratable polls in each city, town, and district of the commonwealth, on the first day of May, shall be taken and returned into the secretary's office, in such manner as the legislature shall provide within the month of May, in the year of our Lord one thousand eight hundred and thirty-seven, and in every tenth year thereafter in the month of May, in manner aforesaid; and each town or city having three hundred ratable polls at the last preceding decennial census of polls, may elect one representative, and for every four hundred and fifty ratable polls in addition to the first three hundred, one representative more.

Representatives, how apportioned.

ANY town having less than three hundred ratable polls shall be represented thus: The whole number of ratable polls, at the last preceding decennial census of polls, shall be multiplied by ten, and the product divided by three hundred, and such town may elect one representative as many years within ten years as three hundred is contained in the product aforesaid.

Towns having less than 300 ratable polls, how represented.

ANY city or town having ratable polls enough to elect one or

Fractions, now represented

more representatives, with any number of polls beyond the necessary number, may be represented, as to that surplus number, by multiplying such surplus number by ten, and dividing the product by four hundred and fifty; and such city or town may elect one additional representative as many years within the ten years, as four hundred and fifty is contained in the product aforesaid.

Towns may unite into representative districts.

ANY two or more of the several towns and districts may, by consent of a majority of the legal voters present at a legal meeting in each of said towns and districts respectively, called for that purpose, and held previous to the first day of July, in the year in which the decennial census of polls shall be taken, form themselves into a representative district, to continue until the next decennial census of polls, for the election of a representative or representatives; and such district shall have all the rights in regard to representation, which would belong to a town containing the same number of ratable polls.

Governor and Council to determine once in every ten years the number of representatives to which each town is entitled.

New apportionment to be made once in every ten years.

THE governor and Council shall ascertain and determine, within the months of July and August, in the year of our Lord one thousand eight hundred and thirty-seven, according to the foregoing principles, the number of representatives which each city, town, and representative district is entitled to elect, and the number of years, within the period of ten years then next ensuing, that each city, town, and representative district may elect an additional representative; and where any town has not a sufficient number of polls to elect a representative each year, then how many years within the ten years such town may elect a representative; and the same shall be done once in ten years thereafter, by the governor and Council, and the number of ratable polls in each decennial census of polls shall determine the number of representatives which each city, town, and representative district may elect as aforesaid; and when the number of representatives to be elected by each city, town, or representative district is ascertained and determined as aforesaid, the governor shall cause the same to be published forthwith for the information of the people, and that number shall remain fixed and unalterable for the period of ten years.

Inconsistent provisions repealed.

ALL the provisions of the existing constitution inconsistent with the provisions herein contained, are hereby wholly annulled.

Senators and representatives, how apportioned.

ART. 13. A census of the inhabitants of each city and town, on the first day of May, shall be taken, and returned into the secretary's office, on or before the last day of June of the year one thousand eight hundred and forty, and of every tenth year thereafter, which census shall determine the apportionment of senators and representatives for the term of ten years.

Senatorial districts.

THE several senatorial districts now existing shall be permanent. The Senate shall consist of forty members; and in the year one thousand eight hundred and forty, and every tenth year thereafter, the governor and Council shall assign the number of senators to be chosen in each district, according to the number of inhabitants in the same. But, in all cases, at least one senator shall be assigned to each district.

House of Representatives, how apportioned.

THE members of the House of Representatives shall be apportioned in the following manner: Every town or city containing twelve hundred inhabitants may elect one representative; and two thousand four hundred inhabitants shall be the mean increasing number which shall entitle it to an additional representative.

Small towns, how represented.

EVERY town containing less than twelve hundred inhabitants shall be entitled to elect a representative as many times, within ten years, as the number one hundred and sixty is contained in the number of the inhabitants of said town. Such towns may also elect one representative for the year in which the valuation of estates within the commonwealth shall be settled.

Towns may unite into representative districts.

ANY two or more of the several towns may, by consent of a majority of the legal voters present at a legal meeting, in each of said towns respectively, called for that purpose, and held before the first day of August, in the year one thousand eight hundred and forty, and every tenth year thereafter, form themselves into a representative district, to continue for the term of ten years; and such district shall have all the rights, in regard to representation which would belong to a town containing the same number of inhabitants.

Basis of representation.

THE number of inhabitants which shall entitle a town to elect one representative, and the mean increasing number which shall entitle a town or city to elect more than one, and also the number by which the population of towns, not entitled to a representative every year, is to be divided, shall be increased respectively by one tenth of the numbers above mentioned, whenever the population of the commonwealth shall have increased to seven hundred and seventy thousand, and for every additional increase of seventy thousand inhabitants, the same addition of one tenth shall be made respectively to the said numbers above mentioned.

Governor and Council to apportion the number of representatives of each town, once in every ten years.

IN the year of each decennial census, the governor and Council shall, before the first day of September, apportion the number of representatives, which each city, town, and representative district is entitled to elect, and ascertain how many years, within ten years, any town may elect a representative, which is not entitled to elect one every year, and the governor shall cause the same to be published forthwith.

Counsellors to be chosen from the people at large.

NINE counsellors shall be annually chosen from among the people at large, on the first Wednesday of January, or as soon thereafter as may be, by the joint ballot of the senators and representatives, assembled in one room, who shall, as soon as may be, in like manner, fill up any vacancies that may happen in the Council, by death, resignation, or otherwise. No person shall be elected a counsellor who has not been an inhabitant of this commonwealth for the term of five years immediately preceding his election; and not more than one counsellor shall be chosen from any one senatorial district in the commonwealth.

Qualifications of counsellors.

Freehold estate dispensed with.

No possession of a freehold, or of any other estate, shall be required as a qualification for holding a seat in either branch of the General Court, or in the executive Council.

[NOTE.—The constitution of Massachusetts was agreed upon by delegates of the people, in convention, begun and held at Cambridge, on the first day of September, 1779, and continued by adjournments to the second day of March, 1780, when the convention adjourned to meet on the first Wednesday of the ensuing June. In the mean time the constitution was submitted to the people, to be adopted by them, provided two thirds of the votes given should be in the affirmative. When the convention assembled, it was found that the constitution had been adopted by the requisite number of votes, and the convention accordingly *resolved*, "that the said constitution or frame of government shall take place on the last Wednesday of October next; and not before, for any purpose, save only for that of making elections, agreeable to this resolution." The first legislature assembled at Boston, on the twenty-fifth day of October, 1780.

The first nine articles of amendment were submitted, by delegates in convention assembled November 15, 1820, to the people, and by them approved and adopted, April 9, 1821.

The tenth article of amendment was adopted by the legislatures of the political years 1829-30, and 1830-31, and was approved and ratified by the people, May 11, 1831.

The eleventh article of amendment was adopted by the legislatures of the political years 1832 and 1833, and was approved and ratified by the people, November 11, 1833.

The twelfth article of amendment was adopted by the legislatures of the political years 1835 and 1836, and was approved and ratified by the people, November 14, 1836.

The thirteenth article of amendment was adopted by the legislatures of the political years 1839 and 1840, and was approved and ratified by the people, April 6, 1840.]

THE

# Constitutional Propositions,

ADOPTED BY THE

# CONVENTION OF DELEGATES,

ASSEMBLED AT BOSTON,

ON THE FIRST WEDNESDAY OF MAY,

A. D. 1853.

AND

## Submitted to the People for their Ratification,

WITH AN

## ADDRESS TO THE PEOPLE OF MASSACHUSETTS.

BOSTON:
PUBLISHED BY ORDER OF THE CONVENTION.
WHITE & POTTER, STATE PRINTERS
1853.

## NOTE.

Amendments adopted by the Convention, which stand as separate articles or paragraphs, are printed in solid form, and enclosed in brackets, to distinguish them from existing provisions of the Constitution. Where an amendment has been made, by adding words to an article or paragraph in the existing Constitution, the amendment is printed in *italics*.

# Commonwealth of Massachusetts.

---

In the Year One Thousand Eight Hundred and Fifty-Three.

---

## RESOLVES.

In the Convention of the delegates of the people assembled in Boston, on the first Wednesday of May, in the year one thousand eight hundred and fifty-three, for the purpose of revising and amending the Constitution of this Commonwealth.

*Resolved,* That the revised Constitution, proposed by said Convention, be submitted to the people of the Commonwealth for their ratification and adoption in the manner following, viz.:—

I. The Preamble. A Declaration of the Rights of the Inhabitants of the Commonwealth of Massachusetts. The Frame of Government, with its Preamble and Chapters numbered One, Two, Three, Four, Five, Six, Seven, Eight, Nine, Ten, Eleven, Twelve, Thirteen, and Fourteen, entitled, respectively, General Court: Senate: House of Representatives: Governor: Lieutenant-Governor: Council: Secretary, Treasurer, Attorney-General, Auditor, District Attorney, and County Officers: Judiciary Power: Qualifications of Voters and Elections: Oaths and Subscriptions: Militia: The University at Cambridge, The School Fund and the Encouragement of Literature: Miscellaneous Provisions: Revisions and Amendments of the Constitution,—as a distinct proposition, numbered "One."

If this proposition, so submitted, shall be ratified and adopted by a majority of the legal voters of the Commonwealth, present and voting thereon, at meetings duly called, then the same shall be the Constitution of the Commonwealth of Massachusetts.

II. The provision respecting the granting of the writ of Habeas Corpus, as a proposition, numbered "Two."

If this proposition be ratified and adopted, it shall be an addition to the provision respecting the Habeas Corpus.

III. The provision respecting the rights of juries in criminal trials, as a proposition, numbered "Three."

If this proposition be ratified and adopted, it shall be an addition to the article in the Declaration of Rights, respecting the rights of persons charged with crimes.

IV. The provision respecting claims against the Commonwealth, as a proposition, numbered "Four."

If this proposition be ratified and adopted, it shall be an addition to Article XI., of the Declaration of Rights.

V. The provision respecting imprisonment for debt, as a proposition, numbered "Five."

If this proposition be adopted, it shall be an addition to the Article in the Declaration of Rights respecting excessive bail and fines.

VI. The provision respecting sectarian schools, as a proposition, numbered "Six."

If this proposition be ratified and adopted, it shall be an addition to Article IV. of Chapter XII., entitled, "The University at Cambridge, The School Fund, and The Encouragement of Literature." If proposition numbered "One" shall not be adopted, the proposition numbered "Six" shall be added as an amendment to the Constitution.

VII. The provision respecting Corporations, as a proposition, numbered "Seven."

VIII. The provision respecting Banks and Banking, as a proposition, numbered "Eight."

If the propositions numbered "Seven" and "Eight" be ratified and confirmed, they shall be added as separate articles, or if either of them be ratified and confirmed, as an article in Chapter XIII., entitled, "Miscellaneous Provisions."

If proposition numbered "One" be not ratified and confirmed, they shall be added as amendments to the Constitution.

*Resolved*, That at the meetings for the election of Governor, Senators and Representatives to the General Court, to be holden on the second Monday of November, in the year one thousand eight hundred and fifty-three, the qualified voters of the several towns and cities shall vote by ballot upon each of the propositions aforesaid, for or against the same, which ballots shall be inclosed within sealed envelopes, according to the provisions of an Act of this Commonwealth, passed on the twenty-second day of May, in the year eighteen hundred and fifty-one, and an Act passed the twentieth day of May, in the year eighteen hundred and fifty-two, and no ballots not so inclosed shall be received. And said votes shall be received, sorted, counted, declared, and recorded, in open meeting, in the same manner as is by law provided in reference to votes for governor, and a true copy of the record of said votes, attested by the selectmen and town clerk of each of the several towns, and the mayor and aldermen and city clerk of each of the several cities, shall be sealed up by said selectmen and mayor and aldermen, and directed to the secretary of the Commonwealth, with a superscription expressing the purport of the contents thereof, and delivered to the sheriff of the county within fifteen days after said meetings, to be by him transmitted to the secretary's office, on or before the third Monday of December next; or, the said selectmen and mayor and aldermen shall themselves transmit the same to the secretary's office, on or before the day last aforesaid.

*Resolved*, That the Secretary shall deliver said copies, so transmitted to him, to a Committee of this Convention, consisting of the President of the Convention, and twenty other members, to be by him designated, who shall assemble at the State House, on the third Monday of December next, and open the same, and examine and count the votes so returned; and if it shall appear that either of said propositions has been adopted by a majority of votes, then the proposition so adopted shall become and be either the whole or a portion of the Constitution of this Commonwealth, as hereinbefore provided, and the said Committee shall promulgate the results of said votes upon each of said propositions, by causing the same to be published in those newspapers in which the laws are now published; and shall also notify the Governor and Legislature, as soon as may be, of the said results; and the Governor shall forthwith make public proclamation of the fact of the adoption of either or all of said propositions, as the whole or as parts of the Constitution of this Commonwealth.

*Resolved*, That each of said propositions shall be considered as a whole by itself, to be adopted in the whole, or rejected in the whole. And every voter shall vote on each proposition by its appropriate number, indicating upon his ballot the subject of the proposition, and expressing in writing or printing opposite to each proposition the word YES or NO; but the propositions shall all be written or printed on one ballot in substance as follows:

CONSTITUTIONAL PROPOSITIONS.

Shall Proposition NUMBER ONE, containing the *Preamble, Declaration of Rights and Frame of Government*, stand as the Constitution of the Commonwealth of Massachusetts?
Yes or No.

Shall Proposition NUMBER TWO, respecting the *Habeas Corpus*, stand as part of the Constitution? . . Yes or No.

Shall Proposition NUMBER THREE, respecting the *Rights of Juries*, stand as part of the Constitution? . Yes or No.

Shall Proposition NUMBER FOUR, respecting *Claims against the Commonwealth*, stand as part of the Constitution? Yes or No.

Shall Proposition NUMBER FIVE, respecting *Imprisonment for Debt*, stand as part of the Constitution? . Yes or No.

Shall Proposition NUMBER SIX, respecting *Sectarian Schools*, stand as part of the Constitution? . . Yes or No.

Shall Proposition NUMBER SEVEN, respecting the *Creation of Corporations*, stand as part of the Constitution? Yes or No.

Shall Proposition NUMBER EIGHT, respecting the *Formation of Banks*, and requiring *Security for Bank Bills*, stand as part of the Constitution? . . . . Yes or No.

*Resolved*, That a printed copy of these resolutions, with the several Constitutional propositions annexed, shall be attested by the President and Secretaries of the Convention, and transmitted by them, as soon as may be, to the selectmen of each town, and the mayor and aldermen of each city, in the Commonwealth, whose duty it shall be to insert a proper article in reference to the voting upon said propositions, in the warrant calling the meetings aforesaid, on the second Monday of November next.

# Proposition Number One.

---

# CONSTITUTION,

OR

## FORM OF GOVERNMENT

OF THE

# Commonwealth of Massachusetts.

---

## PREAMBLE.

THE end of the institution, maintenance, and administration of government, is to secure the existence of the body politic; to protect it; and to furnish the individuals who compose it, with the power of enjoying, in safety and tranquillity, their natural rights and the blessings of life: and whenever these great objects are not obtained, the people have a right to alter the government, and to take measures necessary for their safety, prosperity, and happiness. Objects of government.

The body politic is formed by a voluntary association of individuals; it is a social compact, by which the whole people covenants with each citizen, and each citizen with the whole people, that all shall be governed by certain laws for the common good. It is the duty of the people, therefore, in framing a constitution of government, to provide for an equitable mode of making laws, as well as for an impartial interpretation, and a faithful execution of them; that every man may, at all times, find his security in them. Body politic. How formed. Its nature.

We, therefore, the People of Massachusetts, acknowledging, with grateful hearts, the goodness of the great Legislator of the Universe, in affording us, in the course of his providence, an opportunity, deliberately and peaceably, without fraud, violence, or surprise, of entering into an original, explicit, and solemn compact with each other; and of forming a new constitution of civil government for ourselves and posterity; and devoutly imploring his direction in so interesting a design, do agree upon, ordain, and establish, the following *Declaration of Rights, and Frame of Government,* as the CONSTITUTION OF THE COMMONWEALTH OF MASSACHUSETTS.

---

## A DECLARATION

### OF THE RIGHTS OF THE INHABITANTS OF THE COMMONWEALTH OF MASSACHUSETTS.

Equality and natural rights of all men.

ARTICLE 1. All men are born free and equal, and have certain natural, essential, and unalienable rights; among which may be reckoned the right of enjoying and defending their lives and liberties; that of acquiring, possessing, and protecting property; in fine, that of seeking and obtaining their safety and happiness.

Right and duty of public religious worship. Protection therein.

ART. 2. It is the right as well as the duty of all men in society, publicly, and at stated seasons, to worship the SUPREME BEING, the great Creator and Preserver of the universe. And no subject shall be hurt, molested, or restrained, in his person, liberty, or estate, for worshipping GOD in the manner and season most agreeable to the dictates of his own conscience; or for his religious profession or sentiments; provided he doth not disturb the public peace, or obstruct others in their religious worship.

Religious freedom established.

ART. 3. As the public worship of God, and instructions in piety, religion, and morality, promote the happiness and prosperity of a people, and the security of a republican government; therefore, the several religious societies of this Commonwealth, whether corporate or unincorporate, at any meeting legally warned and holden for that purpose, shall ever have the right to elect their pastors or religious teachers, to contract with them for their support, to raise money for erecting and repairing houses for public worship, for the maintenance of religious instruction, and for the payment of necessary expenses: And all persons belonging to any religious society shall be taken and held to be members, until they shall file with the clerk of such society a written notice declaring the dissolution of their membership, and thenceforth shall not be liable for any grant or contract which may be thereafter made or entered into by such society: And all religious sects and denominations, demeaning themselves peaceably, and as good citizens of the Commonwealth, shall be equally under the protection of the law; and no subordination of any one sect or denomination to another shall ever be established by law.

Right of self-government secured.

ART. 4. The people of this Commonwealth have the sole and exclusive right of governing themselves, as a free, sovereign, and independent State; and do, and forever hereafter shall, exercise and enjoy every power, jurisdiction, and right, which is not, or may not hereafter, be by them expressly delegated to the United States of America, in Congress assembled.

Accountability of all officers, &c.

ART. 5. All power residing originally in the people, and being derived from them, the several magistrates and officers of government, vested with authority, whether legislative, executive, or judicial, are their substitutes and agents, and are at all times accountable to them.

Services rendered to the public, being the only title to peculiar privileges, hereditary offices are absurd and unnatural.

ART. 6. No man, nor corporation, or association of men, have any other title to obtain advantages, or particular and exclusive privileges, distinct from those of the community, than what arises from the consideration of services rendered to the public; and this title being in nature neither hereditary, nor transmissible to children, or descendants, or relations by blood, the idea of a man being born a magistrate, lawgiver, or judge, is absurd and unnatural.

Objects of government; right of people to institute and change it.

ART. 7. Government is instituted for the common good; for the protection, safety, prosperity, and happiness of the people; and not for the profit, honor, or private interest of any one man, family, or class of men: Therefore the people alone have an incontestible, unalienable, and indefeasible right to institute government; and to reform, alter, or totally change the same, when their protection, safety, prosperity, and happiness require it.

Right of people to secure rotation in office.

ART. 8. In order to prevent those, who are vested with authority, from becoming oppressors, the people have a right, at such periods, and in such manner as they shall establish by their frame of government, to cause their public officers to return to private life; and to fill up vacant places by certain and regular elections and appointments.

All, having the qualifications prescribed, equally eligible to office.

ART. 9. All elections ought to be free; and all the inhabitants of this Commonwealth, having such qualifications as they shall establish by their frame of government, have an equal right to elect officers, and to be elected, for public employments.

Right of protection and duty of contribution correlative.

ART. 10. Each individual of the society has a right to be protected by it in the enjoyment of his life, liberty, and property, according to standing laws. He is obliged, consequently, to contribute his share to the expense of this protection; to give his personal service, or an equivalent, when necessary: but no part of the property of any individual can, with justice, be taken from him, or applied to public uses, without his own consent, or that of the representative body of the people. In fine, the people of this Commonwealth are not controllable by any other laws, than those to which their constitutional representative body have given their consent. And whenever the public exigencies require that the property of any individual should be appropriated to public uses, he shall receive a reasonable compensation therefor.

Taxation, founded on consent.

Private property not to be taken for public uses, without, &c.

Remedies, by recourse to the law, to be free, complete, and prompt.

ART. 11. Every subject of the Commonwealth ought to find a certain remedy, by having recourse to the laws, for all injuries or wrongs which he may receive in his person, property, or character. He ought to obtain right and justice freely, and without being obliged to purchase it; completely, and without any denial; promptly, and without delay; conformably to the laws.

Benefit of habeas corpus, secured, except, &c.

ART. 12. The privilege and benefit of the writ of *habeas corpus* shall be enjoyed, in this Commonwealth, in the most free, easy, cheap, expeditious, and ample manner; and shall not be suspended by the Legislature, except upon the most urgent and pressing occasions, and for a limited time not exceeding twelve months.

Art. 13. No subject shall be held to answer for any crimes or offence, until the same is fully and plainly, substantially and formally, described to him; or be compelled to accuse, or furnish evidence against himself: and every subject shall have a right to produce all proofs, that may be favorable to him; to meet the witnesses against him face to face, and to be fully heard in his defence by himself, or his counsel, at his election: and no subject shall be arrested, imprisoned, despoiled, or deprived of his property, immunities, or privileges, put out of the protection of the law, exiled, or deprived of his life, liberty, or estate, but by the judgment of his peers, or the law of the land. And the legislature shall not make any law that shall subject any person to a capital or infamous punishment, excepting for the government of the army and navy, without trial by jury.

Prosecutions regulated.

Art. 14. In criminal prosecutions, the verification of facts in the vicinity where they happen, is one of the greatest securities of the life, liberty, and property of the citizen.

Crimes to be proved in the vicinity.

Art. 15. Every subject has a right to be secure from all unreasonable searches and seizures of his person, his houses, his papers, and all his possessions. All warrants, therefore, are contrary to this right, if the cause or foundation of them be not previously supported by oath or affirmation; and if the order in the warrant to a civil officer, to make search in suspected places, or to arrest one or more suspected persons, or to seize their property, be not accompanied with a special designation of the persons or objects of search, arrest, or seizure; and no warrant ought to be issued but in cases, and with the formalities, prescribed by the laws.

Right of search and seizure regulated.

Art. 16. In all controversies concerning property, and in all suits between two or more persons, except in cases in which it has heretofore been otherways used and practised, the parties have a right to a trial by jury; and this method of procedure shall be held sacred, unless, in causes

Right to trial by jury sacred, except, &c.

arising on the high seas, and such as relate to mariners' wages, the Legislature shall hereafter find it necessary to alter it.

Liberty of the press.

ART. 17. The liberty of the press is essential to the security of freedom in a state: it ought not, therefore, to be restrained in this Commonwealth.

Right to keep and bear arms. Standing armies dangerous. Military power subordinate to civil.

ART. 18. The people have a right to keep and to bear arms for the common defence: and, as in time of peace, armies are dangerous to liberty, they ought not to be maintained without the consent of the Legislature; and the military power shall always be held in an exact subordination to the civil authority, and be governed by it.

Moral qualifications for ffice.

Moral obligations of lawgivers and magistrates.

ART. 19. A frequent recurrence to the fundamental principles of the Constitution, and a constant adherence to those of piety, justice, moderation, temperance, industry, and frugality, are absolutely necessary to preserve the advantages of liberty, and to maintain a free government. The people ought, consequently, to have a particular attention to all those principles, in the choice of their officers and representatives; and they have a right to require of their lawgivers and magistrates, an exact and constant observance of them, in the formation and execution of the laws necessary for the good administration of the Commonwealth.

Right of people to instruct representatives and petition legislature.

ART. 20. The people have a right, in an orderly and peaceable manner, to assemble to consult upon the common good; give instructions to their representatives; and to request of the legislative body, by the way of addresses, petitions, or remonstrances, redress of the wrongs done them, and of the grievances they suffer.

Power to suspend the laws or their execution.

ART. 21. The power of suspending the laws, or the execution of the laws, ought never to be exercised but by the Legislature, or by authority derived from it, to be exercised in such particular cases only as the Legislature shall expressly provide for.

Freedom of de-

ART. 22. The freedom of deliberation, speech and

debate, in either House of the Legislature, is so essential to the rights of the people, that it cannot be the foundation of any accusation or prosecution, action or complaint, in any other court or place whatsoever. bate, &c., and reason thereof.

Art. 23. The Legislature ought frequently to assemble for the redress of grievances, for correcting, strengthening, and confirming the laws, and for making new laws, as the common good may require. Frequent sessions, and objects thereof.

Art. 24. No subsidy, charge, tax, impost, or duties, ought to be established, fixed, laid, or levied, under any pretext whatsoever, without the consent of the people, or their representatives in the Legislature. Taxation founded on consent.

Art. 25. Laws made to punish for actions done before the existence of such laws, and which have not been declared crimes by preceding laws, are unjust, oppressive, and inconsistent with the fundamental principles of a free government. Ex post facto laws prohibited.

Art. 26. No subject ought, in any case, or in any time, to be declared guilty of treason or felony by the Legislature. Legislature not to convict of treason, &c.

Art. 27. No magistrate or court of law shall demand excessive bail or sureties, impose excessive fines, or inflict cruel or unusual punishments. Excessive bail or fines and cruel punishments, prohibited.

Art. 28. In time of peace, no soldier ought to be quartered in any house without the consent of the owner; and in time of war, such quarters ought not to be made but by the civil magistrate, in a manner ordained by the Legislature. No soldier to be quartered in any house, unless, &c.

Art. 29. No person can in any case be subjected to law martial, or to any penalties or pains, by virtue of that law, except those employed in the army or navy, and except the militia in actual service, but by authority of the Legislature. Citizens exempt from law martial, unless, &c.

Art. 30. It is essential to the preservation of the rights of every individual, his life, liberty, property and character, that there be an impartial interpretation of the laws, and Judges of supreme judicial court.

administration of justice. It is the right of every citizen to be tried by judges as free, impartial and independent, as the lot of humanity will admit. It is therefore not only the best policy, but for the security of the rights of the people, and of every citizen, that the Judges of the Supreme Judicial Court should hold their offices *by tenures established by the Constitution, and* should have honorable salaries, *which shall not be diminished during their continuance in office.*

Tenure of the office.

Salaries.

Separation of executive, judicial, and legistive departments.

ART. 31. In the government of this Commonwealth, the legislative department shall never exercise the executive and judicial powers, or either of them: the executive shall never exercise the legislative and judicial powers, or either of them: the judicial shall never exercise the legislative and executive powers or either of them: to the end it may be a government of laws and not of men.

---

# THE FRAME OF GOVERNMENT.

THE people, inhabiting the territory formerly called the Province of Massachusetts Bay, do hereby solemnly and mutually agree with each other, to form themselves into a free, sovereign, and independent body politic or state, by the name of THE COMMONWEALTH OF MASSACHUSETTS.

## CHAPTER I.

### GENERAL COURT.

Legislative department.

ARTICLE 1. The department of legislation shall be styled the General Court of Massachusetts. It shall consist of two branches, a Senate and a House of Representatives, each of which shall have a negative upon the other.

Commencement of political year, and termination.

Art. 2. The political year shall begin on the first Wednesday in January; and the General Court shall assemble every year on the said first Wednesday in January, and shall be dissolved on the day next preceding the first Wednesday in January following, without any proclamation or other act of the governor. But nothing herein contained shall prevent the General Court from assembling at such other times as they shall judge necessary, or when called together by the governor.

Compensation of members.

Length of session.

[Art. 3. The compensation of members of the General Court shall be established by standing laws; but no act increasing the compensation shall apply to the General Court which passes such act; and no compensation shall be allowed for attendance of members at any one session for a longer time than one hundred days.]

Governor's veto.

Art. 4. No bill or resolve of the Senate or House of Representatives shall become a law, and have force as such, until it shall have been laid before the governor for his revisal: and if he, upon such revision, approve thereof, he shall signify his approbation by signing the same. But if he have any objection to the passing of such bill or resolve, he shall return the same, together with his objections thereto, in writing, to the Senate or House of Representatives, in whichsoever the same shall have originated; who shall enter the objections sent down by the governor, at large, on their records, and proceed to reconsider the said bill or resolve: but if, after such reconsideration, two-thirds of the said Senate or House of Representatives, *present*, shall, notwithstanding the said objections, agree to pass the same, it shall, together with the objections, be sent to the other branch of the Legislature, where it shall also be reconsidered, and if approved by two-thirds of the members present, shall have the force of a law: but, in all such cases, the votes of both Houses shall be determined by yeas and nays; and the names of the persons voting for, or against, the said bill or resolve, shall be entered upon the public records of the Commonwealth.

Bill may be passed by two-thirds of each house notwithstanding.

And in order to prevent unnecessary delays, if any bill or resolve shall not be returned by the governor, within five days after it shall have been presented *to him*, the same shall have the force of a law.

Bill or resolve not approved within five days to have the force of a law.

Unless the general court adjourn in mean time.

But if any bill or resolve shall be objected to and not approved by the governor, and if the General Court shall adjourn within five days after the same shall have been laid before the governor for his approbation, and thereby prevent his returning it, with his objections, as provided by the Constitution, such bill or resolve shall not become a law, nor have force as such.

General court may constitute judicatories, courts of record, &c.

Art. 5. The General Court shall forever have full power and authority to erect and constitute judicatories and courts of record, or other courts, to be held in the name of the Commonwealth, for the hearing, trying, and determining of all manner of crimes, offences, pleas, processes, plaints, actions, matters, causes and things, whatsoever, arising or happening within the Commonwealth, or between or concerning persons inhabiting, or residing, or brought within the same; whether the same be criminal or civil, or whether the said crimes be capital or not capital, and whether the said pleas be real, personal, or mixt; and for the awarding and making out of execution thereupon: to which courts and judicatories are hereby given and granted full power and authority, from time to time, to administer oaths or affirmations, for the better discovery of truth in any matter in controversy, or depending before them.

Such courts may administer oaths, &c.

The general court may make laws regulating marriage, divorce, and alimony.

[Art. 6. The General Court shall have power to make laws regulating marriage, divorce and alimony, but shall in no case decree a divorce, or hear and determine any causes touching the validity of the marriage contract.]

General court may enact laws not repugnant to the Constitution;

Art. 7. And further, full power and authority are hereby given and granted to the said General Court, from time to time, to make, ordain, and establish, all manner of wholesome and reasonable orders, laws, statutes, and ordinances, directions and instructions, either with penalties or without; so as the same be not repugnant or contrary to this Constitution, as they shall judge to be for the good and welfare of this Commonwealth, and for the government and ordering thereof, and of the subjects of the same, and for the necessary support and defence of the government thereof; and to name and settle annually, or provide, by fixed laws, for the naming and settling all civil officers within the said Com-

May provide for the election or appointment of officers;

monwealth, the election and constitution of whom are not hereafter in this form of government otherwise provided for; and to set forth the several duties, powers and limits, of the several civil and military officers of this Commonwealth, and the forms of such oaths or affirmations as shall be respectively administered unto them for the execution of their several offices and places, so as the same be not repugnant or contrary to this Constitution; and to impose and levy proportional and reasonable assessments, rates, and taxes, upon all the inhabitants of, and persons resident, and estates lying, within the said Commonwealth; and also to impose, and levy, reasonable duties and excises upon any produce, goods, wares, merchandise, and commodities, whatsoever, brought into, produced, manufactured, or being within the same; to be issued and disposed of by warrant, under the hand of the governor of this Commonwealth for the time being, with the advice and consent of the Council, for the public service, in the necessary defence and support of the government of the said Commonwealth, and the protection and preservation of the subjects thereof, according to such acts as are or shall be in force within the same.

prescribe their duties;

impose taxes;

duties and excises;

to be disposed of for defence, protection, &c.

ART. 8. The General Court shall have full power and authority to erect and constitute municipal or city governments in any corporate town or towns in this Commonwealth, and to grant to the inhabitants thereof such powers, privileges and immunities, not repugnant to the Constitution, as the General Court shall deem necessary or expedient for the regulation and government thereof, and to prescribe the manner of calling and holding public meetings of the inhabitants in wards, or otherwise, for the election of officers under the Constitution, and the manner of returning the votes given at such meetings: *provided*, that no such government shall be erected or constituted in any town not containing twelve thousand inhabitants; nor unless it be with the consent and on the application of a majority of the inhabitants of such town, present and voting thereon, pursuant to a vote at a meeting duly warned and holden for that purpose: *and provided, also*, that all by-laws, made by such municipal or city government, shall be subject, at all times, to be annulled by the General Court.

General court empowered to charter cities.

Proviso.

Each branch of general court may punish certain offences.

ART. 9. Each branch of the General Court shall have authority to punish, by imprisonment, every person, not one of its members, who shall be guilty of disrespect thereto, by any disorderly or contemptuous behavior, in its presence; or who, in the town or city where the General Court is sitting, and during the time of its sitting, shall threaten harm to the body or estate of any of its members, or assault any of them for anything said or done in its session; or shall assault, or arrest, any witness, or other person, ordered to attend it, in his way in going, or returning; or who shall rescue any person arrested by its order: *provided*, that no imprisonment, on its warrant or order, for either of the above described offences, shall be for a term exceeding thirty days; and the governor and Council shall have the same authority to punish in like cases. And no member, during his going to, returning from, or attending, the General Court, shall be arrested, or held to bail, on mesne process.

Limitation.

Trial may be by committee or otherwise.

ART. 10. Each branch of the General Court may try, and determine all cases where their rights, and privileges are concerned, and which, by the Constitution, they have authority to try and determine, by committees of their own members, or in such other way as they may respectively think best.

Each branch to judge of elections, &c., of its members.

ART. 11. Each branch shall be the final judge of the elections, returns, and qualifications, of its members, as pointed out in the Constitution; shall choose a presiding officer from among its members; appoint its other officers; and setttle its rules and orders of proceeding; and shall have power to adjourn, *provided*, such adjournment shall not exceed *three* days at a time.

Adjournment not to exceed, &c.

Adjournment of elections by general court.

ART. 12. And whereas the elections appointed to be made by this Constitution, on the first Wednesday in January annually, by the two Houses of the Legislature, may not be completed on that day, the said elections may be adjourned from day to day until the same shall be completed.

Mode of elections.

[ART. 13. In all elections by the General Court, or either branch thereof, a majority of votes shall be required, and the members shall vote *viva voce*.]

ART. 14. The enacting style, in making and passing all acts, statutes and laws, shall be: BE IT ENACTED BY THE GENERAL COURT OF MASSACHUSETTS. Enacting style.

---

# CHAPTER II.

## SENATE.

[ARTICLE 1. There shall be annually elected by the inhabitants of this Commonwealth, qualified as in this Constitution is provided, forty persons to be senators, for the year ensuing their election; and the Senate shall be the first branch of the General Court. For this purpose the General Court, holden next after the adoption of this Constitution, and next after each decennial census thereafter, shall divide the Commonwealth into forty districts, composed of contiguous territory, and as nearly equal in population as may be: *provided*, that no town or ward of a city be divided therefor. Each district shall be entitled to elect one senator, who shall have been an inhabitant of this Commonwealth for five years immediately preceding his election, and at the time of his election shall be an inhabitant of the district for which he is chosen.]

Senate.

Districts.

Qualification.

ART. 2. There shall be a meeting on the *Tuesday next after the first Monday in November* annually, forever, of the inhabitants of each town and city in this Commonwealth, to be called and warned in due course of law, at least seven days before the day of *such* meeting, for the purpose of electing senators; and at such meetings every qualified voter shall have a right to give in his vote for a senator for the district of which he is an inhabitant.

Manner of choosing senators.

The selectmen of the several towns shall preside at the town meetings impartially; and shall receive the votes of all the inhabitants of such towns present and qualified to vote for a senator, and shall sort and count them in open town meeting, and in presence of the town clerk, who shall make a fair record, in presence of the selectmen, and, in open town meeting, of the name of every person voted for, and of the number of votes against his name; and a fair copy of this

Presiding officers.

Record of votes.

record shall be attested by the selectmen and the town clerk, and shall be sealed up, directed to the secretary of the Commonwealth, for the time being, with a superscription, expressing the purport of the contents thereof, and delivered by the town clerk of said towns, to the sheriff of the county in which such town lies, thirty days at least before the first Wednesday in January annually; or it shall be delivered into the secretary's office seventeen days at least before the said first Wednesday in January; and the sheriff of each county shall deliver all such certificates, by him received, into the secretary's office, seventeen days before the said first Wednesday in January.

Return of votes.

And the inhabitants of plantations unincorporated, qualified as this Constitution provides, shall have the same privilege of voting for a senator, in the plantations where they reside, as town inhabitants have in their respective towns; and the plantation meetings for that purpose shall be held annually on the same Tuesday next after the first Monday in November, at such place in the plantations respectively as the assessors thereof shall direct; which assessors shall have like authority for notifying the *voters*, collecting and returning the votes, as the selectmen and town clerks have in their several towns, by this Constitution. And all other persons living in places unincorporated, (qualified as aforesaid,) shall have the privilege of giving in their votes for a senator, in the town where the inhabitants of such unincorporated places shall be assessed, and be notified of the place of meeting by the selectmen of the said town for that purpose, accordingly.

Inhabitants of unincorporated places.

Plantation meetings.

Assessors to notify.

Selectmen to notify.

[ART. 3. The governor and Council shall, as soon as may be, examine the returned copies of the record, provided for in article second of this chapter, and ascertain who shall have received the largest number of votes in each of the several senatorial districts, and the person who has so received the largest number of votes in each of said districts shall be a senator for the following political year; and the governor shall cause each of said persons, so appearing to be elected, to be notified at least fourteen days before the first Wednesday in January of each year, to attend on that day, and take his seat accordingly.

Governor and council to examine returns.

Notification.

ART. 4. Not less than twenty-one members shall consti-

Quorum.

tute a quorum, for doing business; but a less number may organize, adjourn from day to day, and compel the attendance of absent members.]

ART. 5. The Senate shall be a court with full authority to hear and determine all impeachments made by the House of Representatives, against any officer or officers of the Commonwealth, for misconduct and mal-administration in their offices; but, previous to the trial of every impeachment, the members of the Senate shall respectively be sworn, truly and impartially to try and determine the charge in question, according to evidence. Their judgment, however, shall not extend further than to removal from office and disqualification to hold or enjoy any place of honor, trust, or profit, under this Commonwealth: but the party, so convicted, shall be, nevertheless, liable to indictment, trial, judgment and punishment, according to the laws of the land.

Impeachments.

Limitation of sentence.

---

## CHAPTER III.

### HOUSE OF REPRESENTATIVES.

ARTICLE 1. There shall be, in the Legislature of this Commonwealth, a representation of the people, annually elected, and founded upon the principle of equality.

Representation.

ART. 2. And in order to provide for a representation of the citizens of this Commonwealth, founded upon the principle of equality, every corporate town, containing [less than one thousand inhabitants, may elect one representative in the year when the valuation of estates shall be settled, and, in addition thereto, one representative five years in every ten years. Every town containing one thousand inhabitants and less than four thousand, may elect one representative. Every town containing four thousand inhabitants and less than eight thousand, may elect two representatives. Every town containing eight thousand inhabitants and less than twelve thousand, may elect three representatives. Every city or town containing twelve thousand inhabitants, may elect four representatives. Every city or town containing over twelve thousand inhabitants, may elect one additional representative for every four thousand inhabitants

Representatives, by whom chosen.

Any two towns may form themselves into a district.

it shall contain, over twelve thousand. Any two towns, each containing less than one thousand inhabitants, may, by consent of a majority of the legal voters present at a legal meeting, in each of said towns respectively, called for that purpose, form themselves into a representative district, to continue for the term of not less than two years; and such district shall have all the rights, in regard to representation, which belong to a town having one thousand inhabitants. And this apportionment shall be based upon the census of the year one thousand eight hundred and fifty, until a new census shall be taken.

Based on what census.

Senate to apportion representatives.

ART. 3. The Senate at its first session after this Constitution shall have been adopted, and at its first session after the next State census shall have been taken, and at its first session next after each decennial State census thereafterwards, shall apportion the number of representatives to which each town and city shall be entitled, and shall cause the same to be seasonably published; and in all apportionments after the first, the numbers which shall entitle any town or city, to two, three, four, or more representatives, shall be increased or diminished in the same proportion as the population of the whole Commonwealth shall have increased or decreased since the last preceding apportionment.

Notification thereof.

Representation of new towns.

ART. 4. No town hereafter incorporated, containing less than fifteen hundred inhabitants, shall be entitled to choose a representative.

Cities to be divided into districts.

ART. 5. Each city, in this Commonwealth, shall be divided, by such means as the Legislature may provide, into districts of contiguous territory, as nearly equal in population as may be, for the election of representatives, which districts shall not be changed oftener than once in five years: *provided, however*, that no one district shall be entitled to elect more than three representatives.]

When representatives shall be chosen.

ART. 6. The members of the House of Representatives shall be chosen on *the Tuesday next after the first Monday in November*, annually; but meetings may be adjourned, if necessary, for the choice of representatives, to the next day, and again to the next succeeding day, but no further: but in case a second meeting shall be necessary for the choice of representatives, such meetings shall be held on the fourth Monday of the same month of November.

Towns liable in case, &c.

**Art.** 7. The House of Representatives shall have power, from time to time, to impose fines upon such towns as shall neglect to choose and return members to the same, agreeably to this Constitution.

Qualifications.

**Art.** 8. Every member of the House of Representatives shall have been for one year, at least, next preceding his election, an inhabitant of the town he shall be chosen to represent.

House alone can impeach.

**Art.** 9. The House of Representatives shall be the grand inquest of this Commonwealth; and all impeachments made by them shall be heard and tried by the Senate.

House to originate all money bills.

**Art.** 10. All money bills shall originate in the House of Representatives; but the Senate may propose or concur with amendments, as on other bills.

Quorum.

**Art.** 11. Not less than *one hundred* members of the House of Representatives shall constitute a quorum for doing business.

---

## CHAPTER IV.

### GOVERNOR.

Governor. His title.

**Art.** 1. There shall be a supreme executive magistrate, who shall be styled, THE GOVERNOR OF THE COMMONWEALTH OF MASSACHUSETTS.

Qualification. To be chosen annually.

Tenure of office

**Art.** 2. The governor shall be *a citizen of Massachusetts*, and shall be chosen annually, *by the inhabitants of the towns and cities of this Commonwealth, on the Tuesday next after the first Monday in November.* He shall hold his office for one year next following the first Wednesday of January, and until another is chosen and qualified in his stead. *And no person shall be eligible to this office, unless, at the time of his election, he shall have been an inhabitant of this Commonwealth for seven years next preceding.*

4

By whom chosen.

ART. 3. Those persons who shall be qualified to vote for senators and representatives, within the several towns of this Commonwealth, shall, at a meeting to be called for that purpose, *on the Tuesday next after the first Monday in November*, annually, give in their votes for a governor, to the selectmen, who shall preside at such meeting, and the town clerk, in the presence and with the assistance of the selectmen, shall, in open town meeting, sort and count the votes, and form a list of the persons voted for, with the number of votes for each person against his name; and shall make a fair record of the same in the town books, and a public declaration thereof in the said meeting; and shall, in the presence of the inhabitants, seal up copies of the said list, attested by him and the selectmen, and transmit the same to the sheriff of the county, thirty days at least before the first Wednesday in January; and the sheriff shall transmit the same to the secretary's office seventeen days at least before the said first Wednesday in January; or the selectmen may cause returns of the same to be made to the office of the secretary of the Commonwealth seventeen days at least before the said day; and the secretary shall lay the same before the Senate and the House of Representatives, on the first Wednesday in January, to be by them examined; and in case of an election, the choice shall be by them declared and published.

Power of governor, and of governor and council.

ART. 4. The governor shall have authority, from time to time, at his discretion, to assemble and call together the councillors of this Commonwealth for the time being; and the governor, with the said councillors, or five of them at least, shall, and may, from time to time, hold and keep a Council, for the ordering and directing the affairs of the Commonwealth, agreeably to the Constitution and the laws of the land.

Same subject.

ART. 5. The governor, with advice of Council, shall have full power and authority, during the session of the General Court, to adjourn or prorogue the same to any time the two Houses shall desire; and in the recess of the said Court, to prorogue the same from time to time, not exceeding ninety days in any one recess; and to call it together sooner than the time to which it may be adjourned or prorogued, if the welfare of the Commonwealth shall require the same; and in case of any infectious distemper prevailing in the place where the said Court is next at any time to convene, or any other cause happening, whereby danger may arise to the health or lives of the members from their attendance, he may direct the session to be held at some other the most convenient place within the State.

Governor and council may adjourn the general court, but not exceeding ninety days.

ART. 6. In cases of disagreement between the two Houses, with regard to the necessity, expediency or time of adjournment, or prorogation, the governor, with advice of the Council, shall have a right to adjourn or prorogue the General Court, not exceeding ninety days, as he shall determine the public good shall require.

Governor and council may pardon offences.

Exception.

Not before conviction.

ART. 7. The power of pardoning offences, except such as persons may be convicted of before the Senate, by an impeachment of the House, shall be in the governor, by and with the advice of Council; but no charter of pardon, granted by the governor, with advice of the Council, before conviction, shall avail the party pleading the same, notwithstanding any general or particular expressions contained therein, descriptive of the offence, or offences intended to be pardoned.

Notaries public.

ART. 8. Notaries public shall be appointed by the governor, in the same manner as judicial officers are appointed, and shall hold their offices during seven years, unless sooner removed by the governor, with the consent of the Council, upon the address of both Houses of the General Court.

Coroners.

ART. 9. Coroners shall be nominated and appointed by the governor, by and with the advice and consent of the Council; and every such nomination shall be made by the governor, and made at least seven days prior to such appointment.

Money, how drawn from the treasury.

ART. 10. No moneys shall be issued out of the treasury of this Commonwealth and disposed of (except such sums as may be appropriated for the redemption of bills of credit or treasurer's notes, or for the payment of interest arising thereon) but by warrant under the hand of the governor for the time being, with the advice and consent of the

Council, for the necessary defence and support of the Commonwealth; and for the protection and preservation of the inhabitants thereof, agreeably to the acts and resolves of the General Court.

All public boards, &c. to make quarterly returns.

ART. 11. All public boards, the commissary-general, all superintending officers of public magazines and stores, belonging to this Commonwealth, and all commanding officers of forts and garrisons within the same, shall, once in every three months, officially and without requisition, and at other times, when required by the governor, deliver to him an account of all goods, stores, provisions, ammunition, cannon with their appendages, and small arms with their accoutrements, and of all other public property whatever under their care, respectively; distinguishing the quantity, number, quality and kind of each, as particularly as may be; together with the condition of such forts and garrisons; and the said commanding officer shall exhibit to the governor, when required by him, true and exact plans of such forts, and of the land and sea, or harbor or harbors, adjacent.

To communicate letters, &c., to governor.

And the said boards, and all public officers, shall communicate to the governor, as soon as may be after receiving the same, all letters, despatches, and intelligences of a public nature, which shall be directed to them respectively.

Salary of governor.

ART. 12. As the public good requires that the governor should not be under the undue influence of any of the members of the General Court, by a dependence on them for his support—that he should, in all cases, act with freedom for the benefit of the public—that he should not have his attention necessarily diverted from that object to his private concerns—and that he should maintain the dignity of the Commonwealth in the character of its chief magistrate—it is necessary that he should have an honorable stated salary, of a fixed and permanent value, amply sufficient for those purposes, and established by standing laws: and it shall be among the first acts of the General Court, after the commencement of this Constitution, to establish such salary by law accordingly.

## CHAPTER V.

### LIEUTENANT-GOVERNOR.

Article 1. There shall be annually elected a Lieutenant-Governor of the Commonwealth of Massachusetts, who shall be qualified in the same manner with the governor; and the day and manner of his election, the qualifications of the voters, the return of the votes, and the declaration of the election, shall be the same as in the election of a governor.

Lieutenant-Governor.

His qualifications. How chosen.

[And the lieutenant-governor shall hold his office for one year next following the first Wednesday of January, and until another is chosen and qualified in his stead.]

Tenure of office

Art. 2. The governor, and in his absence, the lieutenant-governor, shall be president of the Council, but shall have no vote in Council; and the lieutenant-governor shall always be a member of the Council, except when the chair of the governor shall be vacant.

Relation to the council.

Art. 3. Whenever, by reason of sickness or absence from the Commonwealth, or otherwise, the governor shall be unable to perform his official duties, the lieutenant-governor, for the time being, shall have and exercise all the powers and authorities, and perform all the duties of governor; *and* whenever the chair of the governor shall be vacant, by reason of his resignation, death, or removal from office, the lieutenant-governor *shall be governor of the Commonwealth.*

Lieutenant-governor to be acting governor in case.

To be governor in case.

## CHAPTER VI.

### COUNCIL.

Article 1. There shall be a Council for advising the governor in the executive part of the government, to consist of *eight* persons besides the lieutenant-governor, whom

Council

Number

the governor for the time being, shall have full power and authority, from time to time, at his discretion, to assemble and call together; and the governor, with the said councillors, or five of them at least, shall and may, from time to time, hold and keep a Council, for the ordering and directing the affairs of the Commonwealth, according to the laws of the land.

Quorum

How chosen.

[ART. 2. Eight councillors shall be annually chosen by the people; and for that purpose the State shall be divided by the General Court into eight districts, each district to consist of five contiguous senatorial districts, and entitled to elect one councillor, who shall hold his office for one year next following the first Wednesday in January, and until a successor is chosen and qualified in his stead.]

State to be districted for the elections.

Qualification.

ART. 3. No person shall be elected a councillor who has not been an inhabitant of this Commonwealth for the term of five years immediately preceding his election.

Mode of election.

[ART. 4. The day and manner of the election of councillors, the qualifications of the voters, the return of the votes, and the declaration of the elections, shall be the same as are required in the election of senators; and the person having the highest number of votes shall be declared to be elected.

Not to hold office or place of emolument.

ART. 5. No councillor, during the time for which he is elected, shall be appointed on any commission or to any place and receive compensation therefor.]

Rank.

ART. 6. The councillors, in the civil arrangements of the Commonwealth, shall have rank next after the lieutenant-governor.

Record to be kept.

ART. 7. The resolutions and advice of the Council shall be recorded in a register, and signed by the members present; and any member of the Council may insert his opinion contrary to the resolution of the majority. This record *shall always be subject to public examination*, and may be called for by either House of the Legislature.

Record to be public.

Council to exercise the powers of governor, in case, &c.

ART. 8. Whenever the office of the governor and lieutenant-governor shall be vacant, by reason of death, absence, or otherwise, then the Council, or the major part of them, shall, during such vacancy, have full power and authority, to do, and execute all and every such acts, matters and things, as the governor or the lieutenant-governor might or could, by virtue of this Constitution, do or execute, if they, or either of them, were personally present.

---

## CHAPTER VII.

### SECRETARY, TREASURER, ATTORNEY-GENERAL, AUDITOR, DISTRICT ATTORNEY, AND COUNTY OFFICERS.

[ARTICLE 1. The secretary, treasurer, auditor and attorney-general, shall be chosen by the people, annually, on the Tuesday next after the first Monday in November; and they shall hold their offices, respectively, for one year next following the first Wednesday in the succeeding January, and until their successors are chosen and qualified in their stead.

By whom and when chosen.

Tenure of office.

The day and manner of their election, the qualifications of the voters, the return of the votes, and the declaration of the elections, shall be the same as are required in the election of governor.]

Mode of election.

ART. 2. No man shall be eligible as treasurer more than five years successively.

Treasurer ineligible more than five successive years.

ART. 3. The records of the Commonwealth shall be kept in the office of the secretary, who may appoint his deputies, for whose conduct he shall be accountable; and he shall attend the governor and Council, the Senate and House of Representatives, in person, or by his deputies, as they shall respectively require.

Secretary to keep records, to attend the governor and council, &c.

[ART. 4. Judges of probate, registers of probate, sheriffs, clerks of the courts, commissioners of insolvency, district-attorneys, registers of deeds, county treasurers, and county commissioners, shall be elected triennially by the people of their respective counties and districts, on the Tuesday next after the first Monday in November, and shall hold their offices, respectively, for three years next following the first Wednesday in the succeeding January, and until their respective successors are chosen and qualified in their stead.

Judges of probate, clerks of court, &c.

By whom chosen.

Day of election.

Tenure of office.

The manner of their election, the qualifications of the voters, the return of the votes, and the declaration of the elections, shall be the same as are required in the election of senators; and the person having the highest number of votes shall be elected.]

Plurality.

---

## CHAPTER VIII.

### JUDICIARY POWER.

Where vested

[ARTICLE 1. The Judicial Power of the Commonwealth shall be vested in a Supreme Judicial Court, and such other courts as the Legislature may from time to time establish.]

Tenure of all commission officers to be expressed.

ART. 2. The tenure that all commission officers shall by law have in their offices, shall be expressed in their respective commissions.

Tenure of judicial officers.

All judicial officers, duly appointed, commissioned and sworn, shall hold their offices *for the term of ten years*, excepting such concerning whom there is different provision made in this Constitution. *And upon the expiration of such term they may be reappointed;* and all judicial officers *for whose appointment a different provision is not made in this Constitution, shall be nominated and appointed by the governor, by and with the advice and consent of the Council, and they* may be removed by the governor, with consent of the Council, upon the address of both Houses of the Legislature.

Removal.

Tenure of present justices.

[ART. 3. The present justices of the Supreme Judicial Court shall hold their offices according to their respective commissions; and the present justices of the Court of Common Pleas shall hold their offices by the same tenure, while the law establishing the said Court of Common Pleas shall continue. All nominations of judicial officers, whose term of office is by this Constitution limited to ten years, shall be publicly announced at least seven days before their appointment: and no person who shall have been commissioned after the tenth day of August, in the year one thousand eight hundred and fifty-three, shall hold by any longer tenure of office than the term of ten years.

Nominations to be announced.

Governor and legislature not to propose questions to supreme judicial court.

ART. 4. Neither the governor and Council, nor the two branches of the Legislature, or either of them, shall hereafter propose questions to justices of the Supreme Judicial Court, and require their opinions thereon.]

ART. 5. The judges of probate of wills, and for granting letters of administration, shall hold their courts at such place or places, on fixed days, as the convenience of the people shall require; and the Legislature shall from time to time, hereafter, appoint such times and places; until which appointments, the said courts shall be holden at the times and places which the respective judges shall direct.

Provisions for holding probate courts.

[ART. 6. Justices of the peace, justices of the peace and quorum, justices of the peace throughout the Commonwealth, and commissioners to qualify civil officers, may be appointed by the governor and Council for a term of seven years; and upon the expiration of any commission, the same may be renewed; and those now in office shall continue therein according to the tenure of their respective commissions: *provided*, that the jurisdiction of the justices named in this article, shall not extend to the hearing or trial of any causes, or the issuing of warrants in criminal cases.

Justices of the peace and how to be appointed.

Tenure of office.

Present justices to continue.

Jurisdiction.

ART. 7. Trial justices shall be elected by the legal voters of the several towns and cities, where, at the time of such election there is no Police Court established by law, who shall hold their offices for a term of three years, and have the same jurisdiction, powers, and duties, as are now exercised by justices of the peace, or such as may hereafter be established by law. Every city or town, authorized as herein provided, shall elect a trial justice, and may elect one additional, for each two thousand inhabitants therein, according to the next preceding decennial census: *provided*, however, that any trial justice who shall remove from the city or town in which he was elected shall thereby vacate his office.

Trial justices to be elected.

Tenure of office.

Jurisdiction.

Number of.

Removal to vacate office.

ART. 8. Justices and clerks of the Police Courts of the several cities and towns of the Commonwealth, shall be elected by the legal voters thereof, respectively, for a term of three years.]

Justices, &c. of police courts to be elected.

Tenure.

---

## CHAPTER IX.

### QUALIFICATIONS OF VOTERS, AND ELECTIONS.

ARTICLE 1. Every male citizen, of twenty-one years of age and upwards, (excepting paupers and persons under guar-

Persons entitled to vote.

dianship,) who shall have resided within the Commonwealth one year, and within the town or district, in which he may claim a right to vote, six calendar months next preceding any election of *any national officer, or any State officer required by this Constitution to be elected by the people, shall have a right to vote in such election; and no other person shall have such right.*

Sealed envelopes to be used.

[ART. 2. All ballots required by law to be given at any national, state, county, district, or city election, including elections for representatives and trial justices, justices and clerks of police courts, shall be deposited in sealed envelopes of uniform size and appearance, to be furnished by the Commonwealth.

Lists of voters to be used at all elections.

ART. 3. Lists of the names of qualified voters shall be used at all elections required by this Constitution. They shall be made out and used in such manner as shall be by law provided. The presiding officers at such elections shall receive the votes of all persons whose names are borne on such lists, and shall not be held answerable for refusing the votes of any persons whose names are not borne thereon.

Day of elections.

By whom meetings shall be called.

ART. 4. All meetings for the choice of national, state, county, or district officers, including representatives, trial justices, clerks and justices of police courts, by the people, shall be held on the Tuesday next after the first Monday in November, annually; and they shall be called by the mayor and aldermen of the cities, and the selectmen of the towns, and warned in due course of law. The manner of calling and holding public meetings in cities, for the election of officers under this Constitution, and the manner of returning the votes given at such meetings, shall be as now prescribed, or as shall hereafter be prescribed by the Legislature.

A majority of votes necessary to the election of governor and other officers.

ART. 5. A majority of all the votes given shall be necessary to the election of governor, lieutenant-governor, secretary, treasurer, auditor, and attorney-general, of the Commonwealth, until otherwise provided by law, but no such law providing that such officers, or either of them, or representatives to the General Court, shall be elected by plurality, instead of a majority of votes given, shall take effect until one year after its passage; and if at any time after any such law shall have taken effect, it shall be repealed, such repeal shall not become a law until one year after the passage of the repealing act; and in the absence of any such law, if at any election of either of the above-named officers, except the representatives to the General Court, no person shall have a majority of the votes given, the House of Representatives shall elect two out of three persons then eligible, who had the highest number of votes, if so many shall have been voted for, and return the persons so elected to the Senate, from whom the Senate shall choose one who shall be the officer thus to be elected.

In case of no election by the people, to be elected by the House and Senate.

A majority of votes necessary in the election of representatives until otherwise provided.

ART. 6. A majority of votes shall be required in all elections of representatives to the General Court, until otherwise provided by law.

City and town officers.

ART. 7. In the election of all city or town officers, such rule of election shall govern as the Legislature may by law prescribe.

A plurality of votes shall elect councillors and other officers.

ART. 8. In all elections of councillors and senators, and in all elections of county or district officers, the person having the highest number of votes shall be elected.

In case of a failure, subsequent trials may be had.

ART. 9. Whenever, in any election, where the person having the highest number of votes may be elected, there is a failure of election because two persons have an equal number of votes, subsequent trials may be had at such times as may be prescribed by the Legislature.]

---

## CHAPTER X.

### OATHS AND SUBSCRIPTIONS; INCOMPATIBILITY OF AND EXCLUSION FROM OFFICES; CONTINUATION OF OFFICERS; COMMISSIONS; WRITS; CONFIRMATION OF LAWS.

Oath to be taken.

ARTICLE 1. The following oath shall be taken and subscribed by every person chosen or appointed to any office, civil or military, under the government of the Commonwealth, before he shall enter upon the duties of his office, to wit:—

Form of oath.

"I, A. B., do solemnly swear that I will bear true faith and allegiance to the Commonwealth of Massachusetts, and will support the Constitution thereof; and that I will faithfully and impartially discharge and perform all the duties incumbent on me as [here insert the office], according to the best of my abilities and understanding, agreeably to the Constitution and laws of the Commonwealth. So help me God."

Persons having conscientious scruples may affirm.

[*Provided*, that when any person, chosen or appointed as aforesaid, shall be conscientiously scrupulous of taking and subscribing an oath, and shall for that reason decline taking the above oath, he shall make and subscribe his affirmation in the foregoing form, omitting the word "swear," and substituting the word "affirm;" and omitting the words "So help me God," and subjoining instead thereof the words "And this I do under the pains and penalties of perjury."]

Before whom taken.

And the said oaths or affirmations shall be taken and subscribed, by the governor and lieutenant-governor before the president of the Senate, in presence of the two Houses *in convention; and by councillors before the president of the Senate and in presence of the Senate;* and by the senators and representatives before the governor and council for the time being; and by the residue of the officers aforesaid before such persons, and in such manner, as shall from time to time be prescribed by law.

Plurality of offices prohibited to governor, etc., except, etc.

ART. 2. No governor, lieutenant-governor, or judge of the Supreme Judicial Court *or Court of Common Pleas*, shall hold any other office under the authority of this Commonwealth, except such as by this Constitution they are admitted to hold, saving that the judges of the said courts may hold the offices of justices of the peace through the State; nor shall they hold any other office, or receive any pension or salary from any other State, or government, or power whatever, *except that they may be appointed to take depositions, or acknowledgments of deeds, or other legal instruments, by the authority of other States or countries.*

Incompatibility of offices.

[No person shall hold or exercise at the same time more than one of the following offices, to wit: the office of governor, lieutenant-governor, senator, representative, judge of the Supreme Judicial Court, or Court of Common Pleas, secretary of the Commonwealth, attorney-general, treasurer, auditor, councillor, judge of probate, register of probate, register of deeds, sheriff or his deputy, clerk of the Supreme Judicial Court, or Court of Common Pleas, clerk of the Senate or House of Representatives; and any person holding either of the above offices shall be deemed to have vacated the same by accepting a seat in the Congress of the United States, or any office under the authority of the United States, the office of postmaster excepted. And no person shall be capable of holding at the same time more than two offices, which are held by appointment of the governor, or governor and Council, or the Senate, or the House of Representatives, military offices, and the offices of justices of the peace, justices of the peace and quorum, notaries public, and commissioners to qualify civil officers, excepted.]

Bribery, etc., operates disqualification.

ART. 3. And no person shall ever be admitted to hold a seat in the Legislature, or any office of trust or importance under the government of this Commonwealth, who shall, in the due course of law, have been convicted of bribery or corruption, in obtaining an election or appointment.

Provisions respecting commissions

ART. 4. All commissions shall be in the name of the Commonwealth of Massachusetts, signed by the governor, and attested by the secretary or his deputy, and have the great seal of the Commonwealth affixed thereto.

Provisions respecting writs.

ART. 5. All writs, issuing out of the clerk's office in any of the courts of law, shall be in the name of the Commonwealth of Massachusetts; they shall be under the seal of the court from whence they issue, and be signed by the clerk of such court.

Confirmation of former laws.

ART. 6. All the laws, which have heretofore been adopted, used, and approved in the Province, Colony, State or *Commonwealth* of Massachusetts, and usually practised on in the courts of law, shall still remain and be in full force, until altered or repealed by the Legislature; such parts only excepted as are repugnant to the rights and liberties contained in this Constitution.

Exception.

## CHAPTER XI.

### MILITIA.

The governor to be commander-in-chief.

Limitation.

His power to call out the militia.

ARTICLE 1. The governor shall be the commander-in-chief of the army and navy *of the Commonwealth, and of the Militia thereof, excepting when these forces shall be actually in the service of the United States; and shall have power to call out any part of the military force to aid in the execution of the laws, to suppress insurrection, and to repel invasion.*

All citizens liable to military service to be enrolled.

[ART. 2. All citizens of this Commonwealth liable to military service, except such as may by law be exempted, shall be enrolled in the militia, and held to perform such military duty as by law may be required.

Militia may be divided into divisions, etc.

Officers to be elected.

Discipline.

ART. 3. The militia may be divided into convenient divisions, brigades, regiments, squadrons, battalions, and companies; and officers with appropriate rank and titles may be elected to command the same. And the discipline of the militia shall be made to conform, as nearly as practicable, to the discipline of the army of the United States.

The governor to appoint adjutant-general, etc.

Tenure of office.

Salary to be in full for all services.

ART. 4. The governor shall appoint an adjutant-general, a quartermaster-general, and such other general staff-officers as shall be designated by law; who shall be commissioned by him for the term of one year, and until their successors shall be commissioned and qualified. And the adjutant-general and quartermaster-general shall have salaries fixed by law, which shall be in full for all services rendered by them in their several offices.

Major-generals to be elected; by whom.

ART. 5. The major-generals shall be elected by the votes of the brigadier-generals and field-officers of the brigades, regiments, squadrons, and battalions of the respective divisions.

Brigadier-generals to be elected; by whom.

ART. 6. The brigadier-generals shall be elected by the votes of the field-officers of the regiments, squadrons, and battalions, and captains of companies, of the respective brigades.

Field officers of regiments to be elected; by whom.

ART. 7. The field-officers of regiments, squadrons, and battalions, shall be elected by the votes of the captains and subalterns of companies of the respective regiments, squadrons, and battalions.

ART. 8. The captains and subalterns shall be elected by the members of the respective companies.

Captains and subalterns to be elected; by whom.

ART. 9. All elections of military officers shall be by a majority of the written votes of those present and voting, and no person, within the description of a voter as hereinbefore specified, shall be disqualified by reason of his being a minor.

Manner of election.

Right of voting.

ART. 10. The Legislature shall prescribe the time and manner of convening the electors hereinbefore named, of conducting the elections, and of certifying to the governor the names of the officers elected.

Legislature to prescribe the time and manner of meetings, etc.

ART. 11. The several officers elected shall be forthwith commissioned by the governor for the term of three years from the dates of their respective commissions, and until their successors shall be commissioned and qualified.

Officers to be commissioned by governor. Tenure of office.

ART. 12. If the electors of the several officers before-named shall refuse or neglect to make an election, for the space of three months after legal notice of a meeting for that purpose, the governor shall appoint and commission for three years a suitable person to fill the vacant office, with the advice of the Council if the vacancy be that of a major-general, or with the advice of the major-general of the division in which the appointment is to be made, if the vacancy be of an inferior grade.

When electors neglect or refuse to make elections; governor to appoint with advice of council; or with advice of major-general.

ART. 13. Major-generals, brigadier-generals, and commandants of regiments, squadrons, and battalions, shall severally appoint such staff-officers as shall be designated by law in their respective commands.

Major-general, etc., to appoint staff-officers.

ART. 14. All non-commissioned officers, whether of staff or company, and all musicians, shall be appointed in such manner as may be prescribed by law.

Non-commissioned officers and musicians to be appointed

ART. 15. All officers of the militia may be removed from office by sentence of court-martial, or by such other modes as may be prescribed by law.]

Court-martial may remove.

## CHAPTER XII.

### THE UNIVERSITY AT CAMBRIDGE; THE SCHOOL FUND; AND THE ENCOURAGEMENT OF LITERATURE.

Harvard College.

ARTICLE 1. Whereas our wise and pious ancestors, so early as the year one thousand six hundred and thirty-six, laid the foundation of Harvard College, in which university many persons of great eminence have, by the blessing of GOD, been initiated in those arts and sciences, which qualified them for public employments, both in church and state; and whereas the encouragement of arts and sciences, and all good literature, tends to the honor of God, the advantage of the Christian religion, and the great benefit of this, and the other United States of America—it is declared, that the PRESIDENT and FELLOWS of HARVARD COLLEGE, in their corporate capacity, and their successors in that capacity, their officers and servants, shall have, hold, use, exercise and enjoy, all the powers, authorities, rights, liberties, privileges, immunities and franchises, which they now have, or are entitled to have, hold, use, exercise and enjoy; and the same are hereby ratified and confirmed unto them, the said President and Fellows of Harvard College, and to their successors, and to their officers and servants, respectively, forever. *But the Legislature shall always have full power and authority, as may be judged needful for the advancement of learning, to grant any further powers to the President and Fellows of Harvard College, or to alter, limit, annul, or restrain, any of the powers now vested in them:* provided, *the obligation of contracts shall not be impaired; and shall have the like power and authority over all corporate franchises hereafter granted, for the purposes of education, in this Commonwealth.*

Powers, privileges, etc., of the president and fellows confirmed.

Power of the legislature declared.

The obligation of contracts not to be impaired.

Power over corporations hereafter granted.

All gifts, grants, etc., confirmed.

ART. 2. And whereas there have been, at sundry times, by divers persons, gifts, grants, devises of houses, lands, tenements, goods, chattels, legacies and conveyances, heretofore made, either to Harvard College in Cambridge, in New England, or to the President and Fellows of Harvard College, or to the said College by some other description, under several charters successively; it is declared, that all the said gifts, grants, devises, legacies and conveyances, are hereby forever confirmed unto the President and Fellows of Harvard College, and to their successors, in the capacity aforesaid, according to the true intent and meaning of the donor or donors, grantor or grantors, devisor or devisors.

Who shall be overseers.

Art. 3. And whereas by an Act of the General Court of the Colony of Massachusetts Bay, passed in the year one thousand six hundred and forty-two, the governor and deputy-governor, for the time being, and all the magistrates of that jurisdiction, were, with the president, and a number of the clergy in the said Act described, constituted the overseers of Harvard College; and it being necessary, in this new constitution of government, to ascertain who shall be deemed successors to the said governor, deputy-governor, and magistrates; it is declared, that the governor, lieutenant-governor, Council and Senate of this Commonwealth, are, and shall be deemed, their successors; who, with the president of Harvard College, for the time being, together with the ministers of the congregational churches in the towns of Cambridge, Watertown, Charlestown, Boston, Roxbury, and Dorchester, mentioned in the said Act, shall be, and hereby are, vested with all the powers and authority belonging, or in any way appertaining, to the overseers of Harvard College: *provided*, that nothing herein shall be construed to prevent the Legislature of this Commonwealth from making such alterations in the government of the said University, as shall be conducive to its advantage, and the interest of the republic of letters, in as full a manner as might have been done by the Legislature of the late Province of the Massachusetts Bay.

Power of alteration reserved to the legislature.

Enlargement of the school fund to two millions of dollars.

[Art. 4. It shall be the duty of the Legislature, as soon as may be, to provide for the enlargement of the School Fund of the Commonwealth, until it shall amount to a sum not less than two millions of dollars; and the said fund shall be preserved inviolate, and the income thereof shall be annually appropriated for the aid and improvement of the common schools of the State, and for no other purpose.]

To be preserved inviolate. Income to be appropriated to common schools.

Duty of legislatures and magistrates in

Art. 5. Wisdom, and knowledge, as well as virtue, diffused generally among the body of the people, being neces-

all future periods.

sary for the preservation of their rights and liberties; and as these depend on spreading the opportunities and advantages of education in the various parts of the country, and among the different orders of the people, it shall be the duty of Legislatures and magistrates, in all future periods of this Commonwealth, to cherish the interests of literature and the sciences, and all seminaries of them; especially the University at Cambridge, public schools, and grammar schools in the towns; to encourage private societies, and public institutions, rewards and immunities, for the promotion of agriculture, arts, sciences, commerce, trades, manufactures, and a natural history of the country; to countenance and inculcate the principles of humanity and general benevolence, public and private charity, industry and frugality, honesty and punctuality in their dealings; sincerity, good humor, and all social affections, and generous sentiments among the people.

---

## CHAPTER XIII.

### MISCELLANEOUS PROVISIONS.

Census.

ARTICLE 1. A census of the inhabitants of each city and town in the Commonwealth, on the first day of May, in the year *one thousand eight hundred and fifty-five*, and on the first day of May of each tenth year thereafter, shall be taken and returned into the secretary's office, on or before the last day of the June following the said first day of May in each of said years; and while the public charges of government, or any part thereof, shall be assessed on polls and estates, in the manner that has hitherto been practised, in order that such assessments may be made with equality, there shall be a valuation of estates within the Commonwealth taken anew once in every ten years at least, and as much oftener as the General Court shall order.

Valuation of estates once in ten years.

Officers to continue.

[ART. 2. Persons holding office by election or appointment, when this Constitution takes effect, shall continue to discharge the duties thereof until their term of office shall expire, or officers authorized to perform their duties, or any part thereof, shall be elected and qualified, pursuant to the provisions of this Constitution; when all powers not reserved to them by the provisions of this Constitution shall cease: *provided, however*, that justices of the peace, justices of the peace and of the quorum, and commissioners of insolvency, shall be authorized to finish and complete all proceedings pending before them at the time, when their powers and duties shall cease, or be altered as aforesaid. All laws in force when this Constitution goes into effect, not inconsistent therewith, shall continue in force until amended or repealed.

ART. 3. The Legislature shall provide, from time to time, the mode in which commissions or certificates of election shall be issued to all officers elected pursuant to the Constitution, except in cases where provision is made therein.

ART. 4. The governor, by and with the consent of the Council, may at any time, for incapacity, misconduct or mal-administration in their offices, remove from office, clerks of courts, commissioners of insolvency, judges and registers of probate, district-attorneys, registers of deeds, county treasurers, county commissioners, sheriffs, trial justices and justices and clerks of police Courts: *provided*, that the cause of their removal be entered upon the Records of the Council, and a copy thereof be furnished to the party to be removed, and a reasonable opportunity be given him for defence. And the governor may at any time, if the public exigency demand it, either before or after such entry and notice, suspend any of said officers, and appoint substitutes, who shall hold office until the final action upon the question of removal.

ART. 5. Whenever a vacancy shall occur in any elective office, provided for in this Constitution, except that of governor, lieutenant-governor, councillor, senator, member of of the House of Representatives, and town and city officers, the governor for the time being, by and with the advice and consent of the Council, may appoint some suitable person to fill such vacancy, until the next annual election, when the same shall be filled by a new election, in the manner to be provided by law: *provided, however*, that trial justices shall not be deemed to be town officers for this purpose.

ART. 6. All elections provided to be had under this Constitution shall, unless otherwise provided, be first held on the Tuesday next after the first Monday of November, in the year one thousand eight hundred and fifty-four.

Art. 7. This Constitution shall go into operation on the first Monday in February, in the year one thousand eight hundred and fifty-four.

Art. 8. The terms of all elective officers, not otherwise provided for in this Constitution, shall commence on the first Wednesday in January next after their election.]

The word "inhabitant" defined.

Art. 9. In order to remove all doubt of the meaning of the word "inhabitant," in this Constitution, every person shall be considered as an inhabitant, for the purpose of electing and being elected into any office or place within this State, in that town, district, or plantation, where he dwelleth, or hath his home.

Provision for preserving and publishing this Constitution.

Art. 10. This form of government shall be enrolled on parchment, and deposited in the secretary's office, and be a part of the laws of the land; and printed copies thereof shall be prefixed to the book containing the laws of this Commonwealth, in all future editions of the said laws.

---

## CHAPTER XIV.

### REVISION AND AMENDMENTS OF THE CONSTITUTION.

Convention.

[Article 1. A Convention to revise or amend this Constitution may be called and held in the following manner: At the general election in the year one thousand eight hundred and seventy-three, and in each twentieth year thereafter, the qualified voters in State elections shall give in their votes upon the question, "Shall there be a Convention to revise the Constitution?" which votes shall be received, counted, recorded, and declared, in the same manner as in the election of governor; and a copy of the record thereof shall, within one month, be returned to the office of the Secretary of State, who shall, thereupon, examine the same, and shall officially publish the number of yeas and nays, given upon said question, in each town and city, and if a majority of said votes shall be in the affirmative, it shall be deemed and taken to be the will of the people that a Convention shall meet accordingly; and thereafter, on the first Monday of March ensuing, meetings shall be held, and delegates shall be chosen, in all the towns, cities, and districts, in the Commonwealth, in the manner and number then provided by law for the election of the largest number of representatives, which the towns, cities, and districts shall then be entitled to elect in any year of that decennial period. And such delegates shall meet in Convention at the State House, on the first Wednesday of May next ensuing, and when organized, shall have all the powers necessary to execute the purpose for which such Convention was called; and may establish the compensation of its officers and members, and the expense of its session, for which the governor, with the advice and consent of the council, shall draw his warrant on the treasury. And if such alterations and amendments, as shall be proposed by the Convention, shall be adopted by the people, voting thereon in such manner as the Convention shall direct, the Constitution shall be deemed and taken to be altered or amended accordingly. And it shall be the duty of the proper officers, and persons in authority, to perform all acts necessary to carry into effect the foregoing provisions.

Art. 2. Whenever towns or cities containing not less than one-third of the qualified voters of the Commonwealth, shall at any meeting for the election of State officers, request that a Convention be called to revise the Constitution, it shall be the duty of the Legislature, at its next session, to pass an Act for the calling of the same, and submit the question to the qualified voters of the Commonwealth, whether a Convention shall be called accordingly: *provided*, that nothing herein contained shall impair the power of the Legislature to take action for calling a Convention, without such request, as heretofore practised in the Commonwealth.]

Specific amendments may be proposed by the legislature.

Art. 3. If, at any time hereafter, any specific and particular amendment or amendments to the Constitution be proposed in the General Court, and agreed to by a majority of the senators and two-thirds of the members of the House of Representatives, present and voting thereon, such proposed amendment or amendments shall be entered on the journals of the two Houses, with the yeas and nays taken thereon, and referred to the General Court then next to be chosen, and shall be published; and if, in the General Court next chosen, as aforesaid, such proposed amendment or amendments shall be agreed to by a majority of the senators and two-thirds of the members of the House of Representatives, present and voting thereon; then it shall be the duty of the General Court to submit such proposed amendment or amendments to the people; and if they shall be approved and ratified by a majority of the qualified voters, voting thereon, at meetings legally warned and holden for that purpose, they shall become part of the Constitution of this Commonwealth.

Legislature to district the State in 1856.

[Art. 4. The Legislature which shall be chosen at the general election on the Tuesday next after the first Monday in November, in the year one thousand eight hundred and fifty-five, shall divide the State into forty single districts for the choice of senators, such districts to be of contiguous territory, and as nearly equal as may be in the number of qualified voters resident in each; and shall also divide the State into single or double districts, to be of contiguous territory, and as nearly equal as may be in the number of qualified voters resident in each, for the choice of not less than two hundred and forty, nor more than three hundred and twenty representatives; with proper provisions for districting the Commonwealth as aforesaid, in the year one thousand eight hundred and sixty-six, and every tenth year thereafter; and with all other provisions necessary for carrying such system of districts into operation; and shall submit the same to the people at the general election to be held in the year one thousand eight hundred and fifty-six, for their ratification; and if the same shall be ratified and adopted by the people, it shall become a part of this Constitution in place of the provisions contained in this Constitution for the apportionment of senators and representatives.]

The same to be submitted to the people.

## Proposition Number Two.

The writ of *habeas corpus* shall be granted as of right in all cases in which a discretion is not' especially conferred upon the court by the Legislature ; but the Legislature may prescribe forms of proceeding preliminary to the obtaining of the writ.

Habeas corpus of right.

Power of legislature.

## Proposition Number Three.

In all trials for criminal offences, the jury, after having received the instruction of the court, shall have the right, in their verdict of guilty or not guilty, to determine the law and the facts of the case, but it shall be the duty of the court to superintend the course of the trials, to decide upon the admission and rejection of evidence, and upon all questions of law raised during the trials, and upon all collateral and incidental proceedings; and also to allow bills of exceptions. And the court may grant a new trial in case of conviction.

Rights of juries in criminal cases.

Duty of the court.

## Proposition Number Four.

Every person having a claim against the Commonwealth, ought to have a judicial remedy therefor.

Claims against the Commonwealth.

## Proposi ion Number Five.

No person shall be imprisoned for any debt hereafter contracted, unless in cases of fraud.

Imprisonment for debt.

## Proposition Number Six.

All moneys raised by taxation in the towns and cities, for the support of public schools, and all moneys which may be appropriated by the State for the support of common schools, shall be applied to and expended in no other schools

Sectarian schools.

than those which are conducted according to law, under the order and superintendence of the authorities of the town or city in which the money is to be expended; and such moneys shall never be appropriated to any religious sect, for the maintenance, exclusively, of its own schools.

---

## Proposition Number Seven.

Corporations. The Legislature shall not create corporations by special act when the object of the incorporation is attainable by general laws.

---

## Proposition Number Eight.

The Legislature shall have no power to pass any act granting any special charter for banking purposes, or any special act to increase the capital stock of any chartered bank; but corporations may be formed for such purposes, or the capital stock of chartered banks may be increased, under general laws.

Banks

The Legislature shall provide by law for the registry of all notes or bills authorized by general laws to be issued or put in circulation as money; and shall require ample security for the redemption of such notes in specie.

---

COMMONWEALTH OF MASSACHUSETTS.

IN CONVENTION, AUGUST 1, 1853.

A true copy of the Resolutions adopted by the Convention, and of the several Constitutional propositions annexed.

Attest,

N. P. BANKS, JR., *President*.

W. S. ROBINSON,<br>
JAS. T. ROBINSON, } *Secretaries*.

# Commonwealth of Massachusetts.

---

IN CONVENTION, August 1, 1853.

The Committee which was directed to prepare an Address to the People of Massachusetts, ask leave to report the form of such Address.

For the Committee,

GEO. S. BOUTWELL, *Chairman.*

# Commonwealth of Massachusetts.

---

## ADDRESS.

*To the People of Massachusetts:—*

The Convention of Delegates, assembled by your authority and directed to revise the Constitution of this Commonwealth, has now closed its labors; and it seeks only to commend and commit the result to your consideration and final judgment. The necessity for the Convention was great, and its labors have been arduous and protracted. As your delegates we have sought for the principles of freedom in the ancient institutions of the State; but we have thought it wise also to accept the teachings and experience of nearly a century of independent existence.

It has then been our purpose to unite in one system of organic law, the principles of American republican institutions, and the experiences of other free States, all contemplated in the light derived from the history and usages of Massachusetts.

And first of all, we think it proper to present for your consideration a complete system of organic law. The present Constitution was adopted in 1780, and there have since been added thirteen important amendments. By these amendments much of the original text is already annulled, and it is only by a careful and critical analysis and comparison, that the existing provisions can be determined. This ought not to be. Constitutional laws should be plain, that they may be impartially interpreted and faithfully executed, "that every man may at all times find his security in them." We have not then thought it wise, or even proper, to preserve, as a part of the

Constitution, provisions which have long since been annulled; nor do we feel justified in proposing new specific amendments, whose adoption will render the fundamental law of the Commonwealth more difficult to be understood, and less certain in its requirements.

We have, therefore, taken what remains unchanged of the Constitution of 1780, and the subsequent amendments, preserving the original language wherever it appeared practicable, as the basis of a new Constitution; and incorporated therewith, such of the resolutions of this Convention as are necessary to give to the whole, at once, a comprehensive and concise character. This has been our purpose; and if our view of duty is correct, we are entirely justified in submitting so much of our work as will give to the people of Massachusetts a complete system of organic law, as one proposition for your adoption and ratification. It is undoubtedly true, that when amendments are specific and not numerous, they should be separately submitted to the judgment of the people; but this mode becomes impracticable in the formation of a new government, or the thorough revision of an old one. Our attention has been necessarily directed to every provision of the Constitution, and but one chapter is preserved in its original form. It only remained for us, either to submit our work, to be added to the old Constitution, as specific amendments, with the conviction that their ratification would render your form of government more complicated than it now is, or else, to embody all of the old and the new that appears necessary to the safe and harmonious action of the system, and present it as *The Constitution of Massachusetts.*

This we now do; and we invite you to consider, that while government is essential to the safety and happiness of each individual, it must necessarily happen that it cannot be in every part alike acceptable to all.

"We may not expect," said the founders of the Commonwealth, "to agree in a perfect system of government: this is not the lot of mankind. The great end of government is to promote the supreme good of human society." We commend the new Constitution to you; not as being perfect, but as greatly to be preferred to the existing frame of government.

It declares the rights and liberties essential to the freedom of the people; it contains, as we believe, a framework arranged according to reason and correct analysis, and it embodies all the fundamental provisions necessary to a just administration of every department of the government.

You will naturally examine with care the character of the changes we have proposed.

We have thought it necessary to make a provision for the purpose of limiting the sessions of the General Court to one hundred days; and to require that the pay of its members shall be fixed by standing laws.

At present, the members of the Senate are chosen by the several counties, which elect from one to six senators, upon a general ticket. We have provided for the division of the State into forty districts, of equal population, and each entitled to elect one senator.

The basis of the House of Representatives has been a subject of careful and anxious deliberation. Differences of opinion existed among us; but a majority of more than one hundred members determined to preserve the system of town representation under which Massachusetts has existed so long and prospered so well. We have then based the House of Representatives upon the municipal institutions of the State, having reference, so far as practicable, to their relative population. By the proposed system, towns containing less than one thousand inhabitants, are entitled to elect a representative for the year when the valuation of estates is settled, and one in addition, annually, for five years, out of every decennial period. Towns having a population of one thousand, and not more than four thousand inhabitants, are entitled to elect a representative every year; towns of more than four thousand, and less than eight, will elect two representatives; towns of eight thousand, and less than twelve, will elect three representatives; while towns and cities of twelve thousand inhabitants, will elect four representatives, and one additional representative for each addition of four thousand to their population. We do not claim that this system, separately considered, is precisely equal; but if it is in some degree favorable to the rural districts, the loss sustained by the large towns and cities is in a fair measure compensated by the manifest advantages accorded to them in the constitution of the Council and the Senate. The inequality of representation between particular towns, when tested solely by population, may, in some cases, apparently be great; but when the rights of different interests and different sections of the Commonwealth are considered in connection with the whole system of elective government, the basis of the House cannot be deemed unequal or unjust. The Senate and Council are based upon population rather than voters, by which the inhabitants of the cities and large towns have influence in these two important departments of the government, quite disproportionate to their just elective power. No human government can attain to theoretic accuracy; and in a state where pursuits, habits and interests are various, it certainly is not the part of wisdom to place unlimited power in the hands of any. We invite you to consider that the governor represents the voters of the State; that the Council and Senate represent population, without any reference to voters, and, as a consequence, that these two departments of the government will eventually be in the control of the cities and chief towns; and finally, that we have sought only to secure to the rural districts, and to the agricultural and mechanical population and interests, a reasonable share of power in one branch of the Legislature. This influence gives to this portion of the people, power to assent to, but never to dictate, the policy of the government. The Convention of 1780 declared that "an exact representation would be impracticable, even in a system of government arising from the state of nature, and much more so in a State already divided into nearly three hundred corporations." We have encountered the same difficulty, and hope that we have overcome it, in our day, as well as they overcame it, in their day.

But our deliberations have not been confined to the proposed system. Many of your delegates are of opinion that the State should be divided into districts, for the election of representatives, according to the number of voters in each. In this opinion a large majority of the Convention do not concur; but we think it our duty, first, to interpret the people's will, and then to give a fair opportunity for its expression upon all questions of importance, whenever such a course is practicable. We have therefore made a constitutional provision, that the Legislature of 1856, under the census to be taken in 1855, shall present a district system, which may be then substituted for the one recommended by the Convention, if, in the judgment of the whole people, it is wise to make the change.

We have also provided that the cities and large towns shall be so districted for the choice of representatives, that no district shall be entitled to elect more than three members.

In the judgment of the Convention, the election of many officers on a single general ticket, is not compatible with the freedom and purity of the representative system.

The property qualification of the governor and lieutenant-governor has been abolished.

The Council has been made elective by the people in single districts, and the records of that body are hereafter to be subject to public examination.

We have provided that the attorney-general, the secretary of the Commonwealth, the auditor, and the treasurer, officers now appointed by the governor or chosen by the Legislature, shall hereafter be elected annually by the people; and that judges of probate, registers of probate, sheriffs, clerks of the courts, commissioners of insolvency, and district-attorneys, officers now appointed by the executive or the courts, shall also be elected by the people for terms of three years.

We have also provided that the justices of the Supreme Judicial Court, and of the Court of Common Pleas hereafter appointed, shall hold their offices for the term of ten years.

In a free government the people should be relieved in a reasonable time, and by the ordinary course of affairs, from the weight of incompetent or unfaithful public servants. Under the present Constitution a judge can only be removed by the difficult and unpleasant process of impeachment or of address. Such remedies will be resorted to only in the most aggravated cases.

Under the proposed system we have no apprehension but that faithful and competent judges will be retained in the public service, while those whose places can be better filled by

CPSIA information can be obtained
at www.ICGtesting.com
Printed in the USA
LVHW08s2102280818
588394LV00011B/995/P

9 780266 262817